W9-CQW-893

SONSHIP

IT'S TIME FOR THE RING & ROBE!

YOU ARE HEIR TO THE KINGDOM OF GOD

SHEPHERD'S ROD

VOLUME XXIII

2018

— 1 Cor. 13:13 —

BOBBY CONNER

Shepherd's Rod Volume 23: SONSHIP - *SHIFTING FROM SERVANT TO SON...*DISCOVERING YOU ARE HEIR TO THE KINGDOM. Copyright © 2018 by Bobby Conner. All rights reserved.
Distributed by: Eagle's View Ministries —A division of Bobby Conner Demonstration of God's Power Ministries
P.O. Box 933 Bullard, TX 75757 USA www.bobbyconner.org
Unless otherwise indicated, all Scripture quotations are taken from the New King James Version. Copyright © 1982 by Thomas Nelson, Inc. Used by permission. Scripture quotations marked AMP are taken from the Amplified® Bible. Copyright © 1954, 1958, 1962, 1964, 1965, 1987 by The Lockman Foundation. Used by permission (www.Lockman.org). Scripture quotations marked Amplified Bible, Classic Edition (AMPC) Copyright © 1954, 1958, 1962, 1964, 1965, 1987 by The Lockman Foundation. (www.Lockman.org) All rights reserved.
Scripture quotations marked NASB are taken from the NEW AMERICAN STANDARD BIBLE® Copyright© 1960, 1962, 1963, 1968, 1971, 1972, 1973, 1975, 1977, 1995 by The Lockman Foundation. Used by permission.
Scripture quotations marked KJV are taken from the King James Version. Scripture quotations marked NRSV are taken from the New Revised Standard Version of the Bible. Copyright © 1989 by the Division of Christian Education of the National Council of the Churches of Christ in the United States of America. Used by permission. Scripture quotations marked RSV are taken from The Holy Bible, The Oxford Annotated Bible, Revised Standard Version. Copyright © 1962, by Oxford University Press, Inc., Division of Christian Education of the National Council of Churches of Christ in the United States of America. Scripture quotations marked GW are taken from GOD'S WORD. GOD'S WORD is a copyrighted work of God's Word to the Nations. Quotations used by permission. Copyright © 1995 by God's Word to the Nations. All rights reserved.
No part of this book may be reproduced or transmitted in any form or by any means, electronic, mechanical, including photocopying, recording, or by any information storage and retrieval systems, without written permission from the author.
Cover Design © Alison Miller Interior Design Printed in the United States of America. ISBN 978-0-9801639-7-1 0-9801639-7-8

CONTENTS

ABOUT THE AUTHOR 5

PREFACE 9
WHAT IS THE SHEPHERD'S ROD?
How and Why I Receive and Record It.

Part One 23
WHAT IS YOM KIPPUR?
Does It Have Value for Us Today?

Part Two 29
DEVELOPING DIVINE DISCERNMENT
Increasing Spiritual Perception –
Hearing and Heeding the LORD'S Voice.

Part Three 45
SONSHIP!
SHIFTING FROM SERVANT TO SON...!
You Are Heir of The Kingdom!

Part Four 75
DECLARE GOD'S GOODNESS
Experience His Loving Kindness – Bask in His Glory!
Psalms 118.

Part Five...**89**

PROPHETIC EVENTS

Prophetic Perspectives and Revelatory Insights.

CONCLUSION..................................... **119**

ABOUT THE AUTHOR
Bobby Conner

Bobby and Carolyn Conner are founders and President of Eagles View Ministries (EVM), a global ministry outreach that focuses on revealing a demonstration of God's awesome power— "Equipping and Empowering the Body of Christ to Take Dominion."

Their goal is to prepare an overcoming generation that transcends gender and age, raising the standard of purity and power to transform nations by expressing the importance of character and integrity in daily life as well as in message and ministry. Sounding the alarm, they are awakening the warriors to arise and contend for the true faith, *advancing the King in His Kingdom.*

Together, Bobby and Carolyn, have a burning passion for spreading the uncompromised message of the Kingdom of God to every nation. Their ministry and mission yield global impact.

SHEPHERD'S ROD 2018: SONSHIP!

Bobby and Carolyn have been married for over fifty-three years. They have two sons, as well as five grandchildren. They have pastored two Southern Baptist churches for over twenty-six years, and they have been ministering for almost five decades in numerous nations across the earth! They are passionate and inspired by a global vision for establishing the Kingdom of God in an authentic demonstration of God's power, knowing that the Kingdom does not consist of mere words, but of *Holy Spirit-empowered* works:

For the kingdom of God consists of and is based on not talk but power (moral power and excellence of soul).
—1 Corinthians 4:20 (AMPC)

Bobby and Carolyn are on a Divine mission to fulfill the Kingdom — empowerment mandate of Heaven.

Their prayer is:

"O Lord, Thy Kingdom Come, Thy Will Be Done on Earth As In Heaven!"

Bobby has authored numerous books and is the writer of many articles for several worldwide journals. He has averaged speaking five times a week for almost five decades. Bobby is a popular guest on several television programs and has numerous teaching videos on the Internet. He is a highly sought after international minister for worldwide conferences. The zeal with which Bobby spreads the message of God's great redemptive power is truly, amazing.

ABOUT THE AUTHOR

Beloved! The following passage has been a guideline for my ministry for these many years. Our focus must be upon Christ.

And I, brethren, when I came to you, did not come with excellence of speech or of wisdom declaring to you the testimony of God. For I determined not to know anything among you except Jesus Christ and Him crucified. I was with you in weakness, in fear, and in much trembling. And my speech and my preaching were not with persuasive words of human wisdom, but in demonstration of the Spirit and of power, that your faith should not be in the wisdom of men but in the power of God
—1 Corinthians 2:1-5 (NKJV)

PREFACE

What Is the Shepherd's Rod?
How and Why I Receive and Record It!

Welcome to the *Shepherd's Rod, Volume 23*! As you begin, please get your Bible and note papers, as I've written much of this book to be interactive with you. You will greatly benefit from looking up the scripture references found in this book. Take your time and digest these life-changing truths. Blessings upon you; as you dig deeper into the destiny God has for your life. Fresh waves of revelatory light will flood your heart and enlighten your spirit as you take time to study your Bible along with this year's Shepherd's Rod.

It's Friday, September 29, 2017, at 7:11 pm, the sun is just setting behind the beautiful Blue Ridge Mountains. The long-awaited Day of Atonement is now upon us. I am blessed to be setting on my porch in our home in Moravian Falls, North Carolina, looking out over the beautiful blue ridge mountains. The sky is golden with the setting sun's rays shimmering upon the clouds which appear to be golden on the bottom and silver on top. There is a sweet soft, gentle breeze stirring the leaves on the trees. It is tranquil and peaceful; I am so grateful and thankful to Father God for His provision.

I can't explain my feelings at this moment my physical body is calm and relaxed. However, within my spirit, there is an expectation and excitement an exhilaration that is beyond human words. I feel as though I could explode! Even after these encounters for over 23 years, it is still spiritually electrifying beyond any human capacity or ability to accurately articulate and explain.

It is almost overwhelming knowing that I will be caught-up into a spiritual realm and a world that is much more real than this one. I will be entrusted with insights more valuable than all the wealth of the world. I am captured between two worlds, the natural and the spiritual. My heart cries out for The Spirit of Truth to reveal all that we need to receive. I am asking God to give me an anointing not to miss a single thing He has prepared for me to receive. I want to help the people of God advance into their victorious future. In a world that in many ways is coming apart, we must have a sure word of hope and assurance. Only Christ Jesus can give us stability in the shaky times.

Just moments ago, the world news was showing the mighty El Capitan mountain in Yosemite National Park has massive rock slides. These rock slides released untold tons of granite rock crashing to the ground below; this is truly a sign that only the foundation of Christ Jesus is our Rock that is sure and stable.

These are some of the most exciting and decisive days in history. Our world is filled with great needs; nations have been ravished by hurricanes, floods, fires, and earthquakes. Day after day we are bombarded with news of another disaster. The need for clear guidance and confident leadership is desperately needed. We must have a steadfast hope founded in the Word of God.

The Body of Christ must be prepared and ready to face the future with boldness and confidence. By the wonderful grace of God for the past twenty-three years, on the Day of Atonement, I've received a vivid visitation from the Lord Jesus. I praise God for His faithfulness to speak to His people.

Let me stress to you these encounters have occurred because of God's great grace and mercy. It's my heart to accurately receive and reveal clearly and precisely what has been made known. So that the Saints of God will be better equipped to grasp the times and seasons that are upon us (see **Habakkuk 2:2**). We must be alert and aware taking advantage of every opportunity God has opened for us. To be uninformed and disengaged can be very costly. God warned that His people perish because of a lack of knowledge (see **Hosea 4:6**).

SHEPHERD'S ROD 2018: SONSHIP!

How Was I Called and Commissioned to Receive the Shepherd's Rod? Let me explain how I was commissioned to receive these encounters; This was not something I was seeking to do. In a powerful encounter, I was commissioned to receive and record the Shepherd's Rod. For these twenty-three years, I've experienced Divine visitations and prophetic encounters with the Spirit of God on the day of Yom Kippur, the Jewish Day of Atonement. I've been sent to distant nations of the world to receive these encounters.

My dear friend, Prophet Bob Jones, received and recorded his Shepherd's Rod visitations, for several decades. Bob was assisted by Paul Keith Davis, Bob would receive the dreams and visitations and Paul Keith would type them out, for clarity. His prophetic reports have proven to be exceptionally accurate and extremely helpful to the Body of Christ.

This experience is as vivid now as it was 23 years ago the moment it happened. Bob Jones, standing in front of me, said to me, "God wants you to start receiving the *Shepherd's Rod*."

I quickly replied, "No Bob I don't want to do this!" However, I did not get to explain my reasons to Bob. Because Bob stated in a firm tone; "well HE wants you to!" He turned around in somewhat of a huff and walked away. I was standing there thinking to myself, man

PREFACE

I did not handle that well, I should have explained to Bob the reasons why I did not want to be involved in the Shepherd's Rod. The reasons were first; I did not want to echo and copy what was already being done. Second, I was not accustomed to receiving revelation like this.

Immediately after my discussion with Bob, I had an experience with the Lord Jesus Christ in which He said, "Bobby, I want you to start receiving and recording the *Shepherd's Rod.*"

I replied quickly, "But Lord, I don't get that kind of revelation." Suddenly, without warning, I was transported upward by the Holy Spirit into an enormous dome-like structure. There were thousands of large screens—much like those you see in a movie theater. On each of the screens, a different scene was being shown. To my total amazement, at that precise moment, I knew every revelation on every screen! Absolutely nothing was not clearly known and understood.

The Lord said, "See! It's no problem for Me to release revelation to you." Then, in a voice filled with awesome authority, He stated, "Yes! I intend for you to obey Me and receive and record the *Shepherd's Rod.*"

In a trembling voice and a yielded heart, I replied, "Yes Lord; with YOUR help!"

Bob Jones and I made a vow and promise never to communicate the content of our *Shepherd's Rods* until they are both in print. We did this to avoid accusations that we had copied each other. It is without question, supernatural that there have been striking similarities between them. The similarities are important because it is in the mouth of two or three witnesses that a thing is established (see **Deuteronomy 19:15**).

Variables affecting the Outcome of Prophetic Proclamations!

Many different variables can affect the timing and or the coming to pass of prophetic words. Our responses and reactions or lack thereof can have much to do with the outcome of a prophetic word. Our actions have alterable effects. We are instructed in Scripture to write the vision make it clear and plain so that people can clearly understand it and move with it (see **Habakkuk 2:2**).

When a prophetic word is given, releasing direction, it is important to seek to obey what God has spoken (see **2 Chronicles 20:20**).

1. **Response**—All prophecy not contained in Scripture is conditional. The word conditional means it can be changed by our response. In many cases, the outcome can be altered by the response or lack of action by the people.

PREFACE

2. **Timing**—The actual timing of when the prophetic word comes to pass may or may not occur in a one-year time frame.

3. **Repentance**—Prophetic warnings may cause either a person or a nation to repent, thus turning away the judgment prophesied. Biblically, this happened when Jonah prophesied to Nineveh, and the city repented, causing God to relent.

Never forget God's promise concerning our prayers have the power to change events:

Then the Lord appeared to Solomon by night and said to him: "I have heard your prayer and have chosen this place for Myself as a house of sacrifice. If I shut up the heavens so that no rain falls, or if I command locusts to devour the land, or if I send pestilence and plague among My people, and My people, who are called by My Name, humble themselves, and pray and seek (crave, require as a necessity) My face and turn from their wicked ways, then I will hear [them] from heaven, and forgive their sin and heal their land. Now My eyes will be open and My ears attentive to prayer offered in this place
—2 Chronicles 7:12-15 (AMP)

Every year the Lord's visitations and revelations are unique—and each year the theme is different, and the subject is diverse. However, the prophetic insights have proven to be continual highly instructive. I pray that

SHEPHERD'S ROD 2018: SONSHIP!

God will release the much-needed insights as well as discernment we so desperately need to grasp the times and seasons we are in.

This year, I was extremely excited when I heard within my spirit, this word was spoken very boldly and strong: "*MOVING TO MATURITY!*" "MY PEOPLE ARE: "SHIFTING FROM SERVANT TO SON!" I will share much more about this important action throughout The Shepherd's Rod 2018. Truly it's high time for the Saints of God to grow up and move into maturity, from servants to Sons (see **Hebrews 6:1**). This truth will greatly aid us in positioning ourselves to accept the inheritance that is ours. As a child of God, we are Joint Heirs with Christ the King.

It's time to grasp the ROBE and the RING!

In these days, much focus must be given to seeking God for an outpouring of Divine Wisdom concerning our true identity. We must overcome the venom and poisonous effects of poor perception. The devil has been extremely active attempting to confuse and sidetrack the Saints, endeavoring to keep them away from their true destiny.

The pathway to discovering this desperately needed wisdom is embracing the Word of God (see **Psalms 119:130**). God's word is our key to unlock our destiny. We are warned that we must become active doers of the Word not merely hearers (see **James 1:22**). Remember faith without works is dead (see **James 2:14**).

PREFACE

Prophetic insights are released to help the Body of Christ discern the times and know what to pray for and what to pray against. I pray that you will take time to pray over and ponder these prophetic proclamations, seek the Holy Spirit's guidance and direction.

God desires to clearly reveal what is coming if we only take time to seek Him, scripture is so true stating: *"My people are destroyed for lack of knowledge."* (see **Hosea 4:6** and **Isaiah 5:13**). Each of us must ask God for open eyes to see what He is showing and open ears to hear what He is saying.

The term "Shepherd's Rod" is taken from **Ezekiel 20:37 (NIV):** *"I will take note of you as you pass under my rod, and I will bring you into the bond of the covenant."* This passage of Scripture symbolically portrays a shepherd holding forth his rod as the sheep pass under it. As each sheep passes before his watchful eye, the shepherd evaluates and inspects each one very closely.

The sheep passing under inspection is pictured in:

Leviticus 27:32 (AMPC): And all the tithe of the herd or of the flock, whatever passes under the herdsman's staff [by means of which each tenth animal as it passes through a small door is selected and marked], the tenth shall be holy to the Lord.

Every true believer is considered one of **"the sheep of *His* pasture"** - **Psalm 100:3**. As His sheep, we also

17

receive a spiritual evaluation at all times not just on the Day of Atonement (see **1 Peter 3:12**). The living Lord Jesus, our Good Shepherd, continues to faithfully watch over His sheep (see **Hebrews 4:13**). He longs to lead us into green pastures; ever seeking to bring us into a deeper understanding of who He is, as well as who we are. We will discover much concerning our Divine Destiny as we seek to follow the Good Shepherd!

I am exceptionally excited to reveal the prophetic revelations that I receive during the Day of Atonement or Yom Kippur. Get ready! God is going to surprise us with His displays of power.

We should be praying and pleading with God to reveal His mighty power. *It's time to get our eyes off the problems and put them on the solution*, which is **Christ Jesus** (see **Isaiah 26:3**). Only then will we have abiding perfect peace.

Let your heart cry out to see God's power.

Let Your work [the signs of Your power] be revealed to Your servants, and Your [glorious] majesty to their children.

And let the beauty and delightfulness and favor of the Lord our God be upon us; confirm and establish the work of our hands—yes, the work of our hands, confirm and establish it.
—Psalms 90:16-17 (AMPC)

18

PREFACE

This plea, "let YOUR work the signs of YOUR power be revealed," must be the cry of our heart. We must desire to see the mighty displays of God's powerful works and the blessing of His anointing upon our hands; this is the pattern set for us by Christ Jesus and the early church:

These signs will accompany those who have believed: in My name they will cast out demons, they will speak in new tongues; they will pick up serpents, and if they drink anything deadly, it will not hurt them; they will lay hands on the sick, and they will get well."

So then, when the Lord Jesus had spoken to them, He was taken up into heaven and sat down at the right hand of God. And they went out and preached everywhere, while the Lord was working with them and confirming the word by the signs that followed.]
—Mark 16:17-20 (AMP)

Scripture teaches that mighty miracles are tools for massive evangelism. Miracles will draw the people to hear and respond to the gospel. As the gospel is preached, expect to see open-air gatherings that bring many into the Kingdom of God.

And a great multitude followed him, because they saw his miracles which he did on them that were diseased.
—John 6:2 (KJV)

19

Again, scripture states that many responded to Christ Jesus when they observed the signs, wonders and mighty miracles which He was doing. This pattern still works today! Miraculous signs and mighty wonders are tools to bring many into the kingdom of God.

But when He was in Jerusalem during the Passover Feast, many believed in His name [identified themselves with His party] after seeing His signs (wonders, miracles) which He was doing.
—John 2:23 (AMPC)

Notice how the New Living Translation records this passage:

Because of the miraculous signs Jesus did in Jerusalem at the Passover celebration, many began to trust in him.
—John 2:23 (NLT)

These above passages reveal that signs, wonders and mighty displays of God's miraculous power are incredible evangelistic tools to win souls for Christ.

Beloved, our goal must be to become active doers of the word of God! It is as we actively lift up Christ Jesus in our lives that people are brought to Him.

Do not be like those who hear but have no heart or desire to fully follow.

PREFACE

But prove yourselves doers of the word [actively and continually obeying God's precepts], and not merely listeners [who hear the word but fail to internalize its meaning], deluding yourselves [by unsound reasoning contrary to the truth].

—James 1:22 (AMP)

CHAPTER 1

WHAT IS YOM KIPPUR?
Does It Have Value for Us Today?

It's A Season of Divine Visitation!

I will answer some of the questions people have concerning these special days such as Yom Kippur. Some might question, "What importance could an ancient day have on my life in this contemporary culture?" You might be asking, *"What exactly is Yom Kippur and what is its value for me and the New Testament church?"*

Before I answer these questions, let us be reminded of Paul's revelatory words:

Now these things befell them by way of a figure [as an example and warning to us]; they were written to admonish and fit us for right action by good instruction, we in whose days the ages have reached their

climax (their consummation and concluding period).
—1 Corinthians 10:11 (AMPC)

This passage reveals the importance of understanding unfolding events in the Old Testament. Seeing that these events have much-needed insights for us aiding and assisting us to better navigate in the end of the age.

Study the Old Testament Events, To Help Avoid Making Some of The Same Mistakes!

We do not want to make some of the same mistakes they made. Scripture teaches their actions can be a template to help guide us to keep us on the right path. Paul reminds us that these events are examples and warnings to us who live in the last days.

Eugene Peterson's Message Bible sheds much light on this passage:

These are all warning markers—DANGER! —in our history books, written down so that we don't repeat their mistakes. Our positions in the story are parallel—they at the beginning, we at the end—and we are just as capable of messing it up as they were. Don't be so naive and self-confident. You're not exempt. You could fall flat on your face as easily as anyone else. Forget about self-confidence; it's useless. Cultivate God-confidence.
—1 Corinthians 10:11-12 (MSG)

PART ONE: WHAT IS YOM KIPPUR?

The New Living Translation states it this way:

These things happened to them as examples for us. They were written down to warn us who live at the end of the age.

If you think you are standing strong, be careful not to fall.
—1 Corinthians 10:11-12 (NLT)

The above verses state that Old Testament events have real benefits for New Testament believers. They help us not to make some of the same mistakes and stumble over the same obstacles during these last days.

Without a doubt, the Body of Christ stands in need of clearer understanding of times, seasons and purposes of God. These special days and their activities have significant benefits and outstanding blessings for us today. In recent years among some Christians there has been a revived interest in the Hebrew calendar, which Moses described in his Five Books as also being God's calendar:

"God spoke again to Moses, saying, 'Speak to the sons of Israel and say to them, "God's appointed times which you shall proclaim as holy convocations/ gatherings – these are My appointed times"
—Leviticus 23:1-2

Notice clearly; God states these are HIS appointed times. God's plans are to reveal His love and salvation to all people (see **John 3:16**).

There is a wonderful resurgence of interest in the Jewish feast days as many believers around the world are rediscovering the Jewish roots of the apostolic faith. There has been rejoicing and celebration over the Hebraic richness of the Scriptures.

Never forget Christ Jesus states that all these are testifying of HIM. The best message ever preached on earth is spoken about in **Luke 24:25-27**, here is Jesus Christ preaching and expounding from the written record of Moses and all the Prophets, speaking of the Old Testament. There could never be a better message than Christ Jesus preaching Christ Jesus.

Then He said to them, "O foolish ones, and slow of heart to believe in all that the prophets have spoken! Ought not the Christ to have suffered these things and to enter into His glory?" And beginning at Moses and all the Prophets, He expounded to them in all the Scriptures the things concerning Himself
—Luke 24:25-27 (NKJV)

Any Biblical ritual has the God-given intent to reveal Christ Jesus to God's people. Yom Kippur is one of seven "eternal feasts" ordained by God in the Old Testament (see **Leviticus 23:14, 21, 31, and 41**). Of the seven feasts, Yom Kippur is the most sacred, a holy season on God's divine calendar and the most solemn day of the Jewish year.

PART ONE: WHAT IS YOM KIPPUR?

It is ordained and designed by God to draw every saint closer to Himself:

*And the L*ORD *spoke to Moses, saying: "Also the tenth day of this seventh month shall be the Day of Atonement. It shall be a holy convocation for you; you shall afflict your souls, and offer an offering made by fire to the L*ORD*. And you shall do no work on that same day, for it is the Day of Atonement, to make atonement for you before the L*ORD *your God.*

—Leviticus 23:26-28 and 29-32 (NKJV)

CHAPTER 2

DEVELOPING DIVINE DISCERNMENT

Increasing Spiritual Sensitivity and Perception!

Hearing and Heeding the Lord's voice!

Never for one moment doubt if God still speaks. One of the most pertinent and important subjects we must study is the fact that God still communicates with His people. It is imperative that we, The Body of Christ, develop a sharper sensitivity to God's voice.

Nothing absolutely nothing, will prepare you and equip you to hear and heed the voice of God's Spirit like *intimacy*. Our goal is to get so close to Christ that He can guide us with His eye (see **Psalms 32:8**).

It is important that we discover how to silence every voice that is contrary to His voice. Christ promises that as followers we have been given blessed eyes to see and blessed ears to hear, to clearly, perceive the ways of God (see **Matthew 13:16-17**).

Scripture states the hearing ear and the seeing eye the Lord has created (see **Proverbs 20:12**). None of us want to remain dull of hearing (see **Matthew 13:18 and Hebrews 5:11**). We want to become extremely sensitive to the faintest whisper of God's voice, being attuned to all things the Holy Spirit is communicating. Only then will we be building upon, a firm and stable foundation.

It Is Foolish to Build with A Faulty Foundation

Christ Jesus states a tremendously strong warning concerning our need to hear and obey His words:

"So everyone who hears these words of Mine and acts on them, will be like a wise man [a far-sighted, practical, and sensible man] who built his house on the rock. And the rain fell, and the floods and torrents came, and the winds blew and slammed against that house; yet it did not fall, because it had been founded on the rock. And everyone who hears these words of Mine and does not do them, will be like a foolish (stupid) man who built his house on the sand. And the rain fell, and the floods and torrents came, and the winds blew and slammed against that house; and it fell—and great and complete was its fall."

When Jesus had finished [speaking] these words [on the mountain], the crowds were astonished and overwhelmed at His teaching; for He was teaching them as one who had authority [to teach entirely of His own volition], and not as their scribes [who relied on others to confirm their authority].
—Matthew 7:24-29 (AMP)

PART TWO: DIVINE DISCERNMENT!

Globally we see dark and dangerous days. It is imperative that we have eyes to see and ears to hear, we must develop clear reception and precise perception. Scripture states: *My people are destroyed for lack of knowledge* (see **Hosea 4:6**).

It is as we obey the Word of God that our lives are built and established on the solid rock of Christ Jesus and His word.

Before I commence describing my encounters with the Lord during this Yom Kippur season. I'd like to address a question that may be on many readers' mind. You may be wondering whether God really does speak so directly and clearly to believers. In other words, are these encounters Biblical? Can we actually hear the voice of the Spirit and see the realms of heaven today, just like in Biblical times? Let me encourage you, the Lord Himself states that you can hear the voice of God (see **John 10:3, 27**).

Yes—emphatically, yes; this is the inheritance of every believer! In fact, to obtain for us this sublime intimacy and reconciliation with our Father is the reason the Lord Jesus Christ went to Calvary. God's promise to us as our Father is sounded out clearly and strongly in God's Word: *The Lord's sheep will hear His voice.*

Thank God that He still speaks today and that He passionately desires to have intimate fellowship with us.

God also promises that He will reveal *"things to come"* events that will unfold in our future to every believer through the Holy Spirit.

Consider the Lord's promise to us in the Gospel of John:

But when He, the Spirit of Truth (the Truth-giving Spirit) comes, He will guide you into all the Truth (the whole, full Truth). For He will not speak His own message [on His own authority]; but He will tell whatever He hears [from the Father; He will give the message that has been given to Him], and He will announce and declare to you the things that are to come [that will happen in the future].
—John 16:13 (AMPC)

Ask for revelatory insights as you study these pages; let the Holy Spirit guide you into the deep and wonderful manna from the Father's heart.

"You [also] gave Your good Spirit to instruct them, You did not withhold Your manna from their mouth, And You gave them water for their thirst.
—Nehemiah 9:20 (AMP)

If you ask for wisdom, the Holy Spirit will release understanding into your spirit (see **James 1:5**). I was told knowledge without wisdom is worthless. However, knowledge with Godly wisdom is priceless. It is a pearl of great price.

PART TWO: DIVINE DISCERNMENT!

The Lord Jesus states these promises concerning the Holy Spirit:

But the Comforter (Counselor, Helper, Intercessor, Advocate, Strengthener, Standby), the Holy Spirit, Whom the Father will send in My name [in My place, to represent Me and act on My behalf], He will teach you all things. And He will cause you to recall (will remind you of, bring to your remembrance) everything I have told you.
—John 14:26 (AMPC)

Ponder each of these remarkable titles revealed for the Holy Spirit; this will help you understand how adequate HE is to meet all needs within our life. HE is our:

- *Comforter*
- *Counselor*
- *Helper*
- *Intercessor*
- *Advocate*
- *Strengthener*
- *Standby*

We must not merely hear the Word of God; we are also called to obey, surrendering our lives to its directions. Walking in victory requires action to the Word and the way of God. Nothing is more important than obedience!

33

But be doers of the word, and not hearers only, deceiving yourselves. For if anyone is a hearer of the word and not a doer, he is like a man observing his natural face in a mirror; for he observes himself, goes away, and immediately forgets what kind of man he was.

But he who looks into the perfect law of liberty and continues in it, and is not a forgetful hearer but a doer of the work, this one will be blessed in what he does.
—James 1:22-25 (NKJV)

It's my earnest prayer that the Lord would help each of us to hear His voice more clearly, and that He would give us the grace to obey—to obey swiftly, without hesitation. The happiest and most contented people I know are the ones that swiftly and completely obey the voice of the Lord. Never forget rebellion is as the sin of witchcraft (see **1 Samuel 15:23**)!

It is exceedingly difficult to convey supernatural events with natural vocabulary. Our words are extremely weak when called upon to describe spiritual realms and ideas; for this reason, our dependence must be upon the Spirit of God. Only the Spirit of Truth can convey the true message.

It is marvelous to grasp the concept that at the moment of conversion God gave you a heart that can respond to Him and His ways:

A new heart will I give you and a new spirit will I put within you, and I will take away the stony heart out

of your flesh and give you a heart of flesh. And I will put my Spirit within you and cause you to walk in My statutes, and you shall heed My ordinances and do them.
—Ezekiel 36:26-27 (AMPC)

Join in Paul's prayer that the eyes of your heart will be flooded with revelatory light so that you may have insight regarding the works that the Holy Spirit is doing.

[For I always pray to] the God of our Lord Jesus Christ, the Father of glory, that He may grant you a spirit of wisdom and revelation [of insight into mysteries and secrets] in the [deep and intimate] knowledge of Him,

By having the eyes of your heart flooded with light, so that you can know and understand the hope to which He has called you, and how rich is His glorious inheritance in the saints (His set-apart ones),

And [so that you can know and understand] what is the immeasurable and unlimited and surpassing greatness of His power in and for us who believe, as demonstrated in the working of His mighty strength,
—Ephesians 1:17-19 (AMPC)

Each of us should seek to obtain these promises of this prayer:

—Receive a spirit of wisdom and revelation!
—Receive insight into mysteries and divine secrets!

35

—Receive deep and intimate knowledge of God!
—Receive understanding of the greatness of God's power!

THE LORD'S SHEEP HEAR HIS VOICE!

To him the doorkeeper opens, and the sheep hear his voice; and he calls his own sheep by name and leads them out. And when he brings out his own sheep, he goes before them; and the sheep follow him, for they know his voice. Yet they will by no means follow a stranger, but will flee from him, for they do not know the voice of strangers.
—John 10:3-5 (NKJV)

During these turbulent transitional times, it is crucial that we embrace the Lord's promise given to us in —**John 10:27**: *"My sheep hear My voice, and I know them, and they follow Me."*

Ponder these points:

1. Relationship — *"My sheep!"*
2. Reception — *"***hear** *My voice!"*
3. Recognized — *"and I know them!"*
4. Responsibility — *"and they follow Me!"*

Each one of us should earnestly pray and ask God to remove anything that would hinder us from clearly hearing and completely heeding and obeying His voice.

36

PART TWO: DIVINE DISCERNMENT!

Lay hold of this powerful promise:

But blessed [spiritually aware, and favored by God] are your eyes, because they see; and your ears, because they hear. I assure you and most solemnly say to you, many prophets and righteous men [who were honorable and in right standing with God] longed to see what you see, and did not see it, and to hear what you hear, and did not hear it.

—**Matthew 13:16-17 (AMP)**

We have blessed ears and blessed eyes; capable of hearing and seeing revealed truth. Without a doubt, we need keener *perception* and clearer *reception*. Make a firm commitment to fully follow the Lamb wherever He leads, never forget He leads us in the paths of righteousness for His name sake (see **Psalms 23:3**).

Pray this prayer:

Wonderful Lord thank YOU for Your tender mercies and great goodness. Please open my spiritual eyes to see You and Your Kingdom. Unstop my spiritual ears to hear all that You say. Give me the grace to obey swiftly, with boldness like a lion.

Release to me the higher, divine wisdom I need to navigate these end times. I ask You, Living God, to release breakthrough! Lord, restore hope, within all hearts! Lord keep me firmly focused, upon YOU! Amen!

May we never be guilty of these shocking, scandalous words recorded against these people living in Ezekiel's day. We don't want to be rebellious, dull and dumb concerning the Word of Almighty God.

The word of the Lord also came to me, saying,

Son of man, you dwell in the midst of the house of the rebellious, who have eyes to see and see not, who have ears to hear and hear not, for they are a rebellious house.
—Ezekiel 12:1-2 (AMPC)

It is heartbreaking that so many in our day, with a contaminated compromising culture, are guilty of making the very same statement in their lifestyle and actions.

Never forget our deeds speak louder than our words.

"Yet they say to God, 'Depart from us, For we do not desire the knowledge of Your ways.

'Who [and what] is the Almighty, that we should serve Him? And what would we gain if we plead with Him?
—Job 21:14-15 (AMP)

In these dark and dangerous days, it is imperative that we get into the Word of God, and get the Word of God into us, allowing it to become a bright lamp to our feet and a light to our path. Don't stumble about in the darkness it's time to run to the light.

PART TWO: DIVINE DISCERNMENT!

Your word is a lamp to my feet and a light to my path.
—Psalm 119:105 (AMPC)

As we yield our life to the guidelines of the Word of God, we will discover clear wisdom and gain a clear understanding of our life's direction.

The unfolding of Your [glorious] words give light; Their unfolding gives understanding to the simple (childlike).
—Psalm 119:130 (AMP)

The Christian life is not lived stumbling and groping about in the darkness but walking confidently and boldly in the light!

This is the message [of God's promised revelation] which we have heard from Him and now announce to you, that God is Light [He is holy, His message is truthful, He is perfect in righteousness], and in Him there is no darkness at all [no sin, no wickedness, no imperfection]. If we say that we have fellowship with Him and yet walk in the darkness [of sin], we lie and do not practice the truth; but if we [really] walk in the Light [that is, live each and every day in conformity with the precepts of God], as He Himself is in the Light, we have [true, unbroken] fellowship with one another [He with us, and we with Him], and the blood of Jesus His Son cleanses us from all sin [by erasing the stain of sin, keeping us cleansed from sin in all its forms and manifestations]. If we say we have no sin [refusing to admit that we are sinners], we

39

delude ourselves and the truth is not in us. [His word does not live in our hearts.] If we [freely] admit that we have sinned and confess our sins, He is faithful and just [true to His own nature and promises], and will forgive our sins and cleanse us continually from all unrighteousness [our wrongdoing, everything not in conformity with His will and purpose]. If we say that we have not sinned [refusing to admit acts of sin], we make Him [out to be] a liar [by contradicting Him] and His word is not in us.
—1 John 1:5–10 (AMP)

Scripture clearly warns us that during these days it is going to get much darker in this wicked world, but for the children of God, it will get lighter and brighter as we choose to walk in the radiant brilliance of God's revealed glory.

"Arise [from spiritual depression to a new life], shine [be radiant with the glory and brilliance of the LORD]; for your light has come, And the glory and brilliance of the LORD has risen upon you.

"For in fact, darkness will cover the earth And deep darkness will cover the peoples; But the LORD will rise upon you [Jerusalem] And His glory and brilliance will be seen on you.

"Nations will come to your light, And kings to the brightness of your rising.

PART TWO: DIVINE DISCERNMENT!

"Lift up your eyes around you and see; They all gather together, they come to you. Your sons will come from far away, And your daughters will be looked after at their side.

"Then you will see and be radiant, And your heart will tremble [with joy] and rejoice Because the abundant wealth of the seas will be brought to you,

The wealth of the nations will come to you. "A multitude of camels [from the eastern trading tribes] will cover you [Jerusalem], The young camels of Midian and Ephah; All those from Sheba [who once came to trade] will come Bringing gold and frankincense And proclaiming the praises of the LORD.

—Isaiah 60:1–6 (AMP)

Beloved! We are living in unprecedented times; never before has there been such an opportunity for advancing the Kingdom of God. Spreading the good news of the Gospel of Christ must become our main goal. God's plan is to fill the entire earth with the Glory of Jesus.

Never forget we must keep the main thing the *"main thing!"* That is winning souls for Christ. The Church truly stands at an open door, and the Lord has extended His invitation for us to come up higher! There is an increasing hunger growing within the hearts of many within the Church.

Be confident of this fact: *if we seek God with all our heart, we will have a divine connection* (see **Jeremiah 29:12-13**).

Answer God's Invitation to Come Near

After this I looked, and behold, a door standing open in heaven! And the first voice which I had heard, like the sound of a [war] trumpet speaking with me, said, "Come up here, and I will show you what must take place after these things."

At once I was in [special communication with] the Spirit; and behold, a throne stood in heaven, with One seated on the throne.

And He who sat there appeared like [the crystalline sparkle of] a jasper stone and [the fiery redness of] a sardius stone, and encircling the throne there was a rainbow that looked like [the color of an] emerald.

Twenty-four [other] thrones surrounded the throne; and seated on these thrones were twenty-four elders dressed in white clothing, with crowns of gold on their heads.
—Revelation 4:1–4 (AMP)

It's time to answer God's invitation to draw near!

PART TWO: DIVINE DISCERNMENT!

What Do You See Coming?

"Some of the Best of Times!" And Some of the worst of Times!"

I am asked this question countless times. People are desperate to know what is unfolding in the days before us. My answer is; *"it is going to be the best of times and the worst of times!"* The Seers and Watchman of our day must declare what is coming in order to prepare the people of God. We will see some of the best of times and some of the worst of times. The factor determining what we behold is what we have set our hearts upon! If we are busy serving the flesh and neglecting the Spirit, expect disappointment and despair, however, if we have set our heart upon the King of Glory, expect overwhelming joy and victories.

"Watchman, what of the night? Watchman, what of the night? The watchman said, The morning cometh, and also the night..."
—Isaiah 21:11–12 (KJV)

Notice in these verses, a question is asked of the *Watchman* the word used here is a word for "guard, one who watches to protect" what of the night, in other words, what's taking place? These verses speak of two things occurring in the same season. Just as the prophet reported about the night and the light appearing at the same time, these days also will be days of great contrast: joy and sorrow, jubilation

43

and depression, life and death, peace and anarchy. Don't forget God has given us the responsibility to choose by our actions what we receive (see **Deuteronomy 30:15-20**).

Our response to God's guidance will greatly determine the outcome. Don't settle for less than God's perfect will for your life. God states His plans for you are good, to give you a good, noble life (see **Jeremiah 29:11**). And a life filled with hope and a bright future (see **Jeremiah 31:17**).

The Spirit of God is calling each of us to behold the Beloved in His glory. It is time to view the victorious King. The more we know about HIM, the more we will understand who we are to be.

And all of us, as with unveiled face, [because we] continued to behold [in the Word of God] as in a mirror the glory of the Lord, are constantly being transfigured into His very own image in ever increasing splendor and from one degree of glory to another; [for this comes] from the Lord [Who is] the Spirit.
—2 Corinthians 3:18 (AMPC)

Make it your quest to remove every veil and hindrance that would keep you from beholding the risen King in His Glory!

CHAPTER 3

SONSHIP! SHIFTING FROM SERVANT TO SON...!
You are Heir to the Kingdom of God!

For all who are allowing themselves to be led by the Spirit of God are sons of God.
                    —Romans 8:14 (AMP)

It's time for the RING and the ROBE!

An Encounter with The Devil

First, let me strongly stress and firmly emphasize never at any time under any circumstance seek or attempt to institute or instigate an encounter with evil in any form! In the realm of the spirit, I received a visitation from the devil himself. I will share with you some things I've learned concerning the devil. After this encounter with him, I am totally convinced the message most hated and feared by all hell is the true message of *Divine Sonship*. The forces of darkness do all they can to deceive God's people!

Especially attempting to keep Saints from understanding their position and destiny causing them to be confused concerning who they are in Christ.

In over 48 years of ministering I've had untold encounters with the spirit realm both *Holy* as well as *hellish*. However, I have only seen satan twice. In one of these encounters I was suddenly approached by the devil, he came winsome and handsome. He did not appear in a flaming suit of fire, there were no horns on his head or pitchfork in his hands, quite the contrary he was brilliant and stunningly beautiful, yet reeking with evil wickedness beyond human words to describe.

His appearance should not surprise us, remember scripture informs and warns that satan can seek to appear as an angel of light.

And no wonder! For Satan himself transforms himself into an angel of light.
—2 Corinthians 11:14 (NKJV)

In this evil event, the devil in the most convincing tone said to me; "I will give you all these; gesturing with the moving of his hands, in a sweeping panoramic view, revealing the kingdoms and riches of the world!" He stated in a pleasant and especially persuasive and compelling tone and tenor; "these (the kingdoms and riches), can all be yours if you will abandon the message of "Divine Sonship!"

PART THREE: SONSHIP!

The hostility and hatred in the tone of his voice as he spoke of Sonship was tangible.

Notice this is also the similar manner the evil one spoke to our Lord Jesus:

Again, the devil took Him up on a very high mountain and showed Him all the kingdoms of the world and the glory [splendor, magnificence, and excellence] of them; and he said to Him, "All these things I will give You, if You fall down and worship me." Then Jesus said to him, "Go away, Satan! For it is written and forever remains written, 'You shall worship the Lord your God, and serve Him only. "'Then the devil left Him; and angels came and ministered to Him [bringing Him food and serving Him].
—Matthew 4:8-11 (AMP)

After hearing his diabolical and deceitful offer in this encounter, out of my mouth came these words; *"you are a liar, I rebuke you in the name of JESUS CHRIST, and command you to leave."* To which he had to obey! In what sounded like a loud clap of thunder He was instantly gone.

Remember scripture states that if we resist the devil, *he will flee from us.*

The Word of God teaches us that while we are walking in obedience to the Word of God and yielded to God's way we have authority.

So submit to [the authority of] God. Resist the devil [stand firm against him] and he will flee from you.
—James 4:7 (AMP)

Never doubt you can and should be bold and confident as a Believer in Christ. You have within you more power than all the combined evil hordes of hell!

Little children (believers, dear ones), you are of God and you belong to Him and have [already] overcome them [the agents of the antichrist]; because He who is in you is greater than he (Satan) who is in the world [of sinful mankind].
—1 John 4:4 (AMP)

In the Message Bible, we are assured that the battle is already won!

My dear children, you come from God and belong to God. You have already won a big victory over those false teachers, for the Spirit in you is far stronger than anything in the world...
—1 John 4:4 (MSG)

Knowing that we've been given authority to override the devil's ability (see **Luke 10:19**). It is time to stand your ground and take authority and control. You have by Christ Jesus been anointed as Kings and Priests (see **Revelations 1:5-6**). We must grasp the power we have been entrusted to legislate in the spiritual realm. Scripture states we are the Senior Representatives of Christ, sent out into the

PART THREE: SONSHIP!

Kingdom to wheel authority (see **2 Corinthians 5:20**). Jesus said what we bind on earth will be bound for us in heaven, it is time to stand up and bind-up the works of the devil (see **Matthew 18:18**).

The seventy returned with joy, saying, "Lord, even the demons are subject to us in Your name." He said to them, "I watched Satan fall from heaven like [a flash of] lightning. Listen carefully: I have given you authority [that you now possess] to tread on serpents and scorpions, and [the ability to exercise authority] over all the power of the enemy (Satan); and nothing will [in any way] harm you. Nevertheless do not rejoice at this, that the spirits are subject to you, but rejoice that your names are recorded in heaven."
—Luke 10:17-20 (AMP)

Let the words of Christ spoken to His disciples encourage and empower you. Christ is the same yesterday today and forever! It is as we walk in the peace and protection of Christ, our Conquering King, that the God of Peace crushes satan under our feet.

The God of peace will soon crush Satan under your feet The [wonderful] grace of our Lord Jesus be with you.
—Romans 16:20 (AMP)

One of the most important things I realized from this encounter is; I am certain we must focus, giving earnest heed to maturing the Saints, to learn and lay hold of this message of SONSHIP. Anything the devil wants, I want right the opposite!

Sonship is The Message – *The devil and All Hell Hates!*

Beloved! Please believe me when I say the devil hates the message of Sonship! The Saints of God must ascertain and absorb the message and meaning of Sonship so that we can better grasp its power to transform God's people into moving from a mentality of mere servants to Sons of Almighty God.

In these days of releasing revelatory insights, we will discover more concerning our inheritance and what it means to be joint heirs with Christ Jesus (see **Romans 8:17**). By the finished work of Christ our King, we have been made Priests and Kings (see **Revelation 1:5-6**)!

Never let anything rob you of your Divine destiny!

Divine Sonship is a powerful and promising message! The Saints of God must comprehend their true identity. This revelation will release a boldness and confidence that will be life-changing. Knowing it is Christ in us the assurance of glorious victory (see **Colossians 1:27**). God is on our side we will not be defeated or put to shame.

PART THREE: SONSHIP!

The Lord is for me, so I will have no fear. What can mere people do to me?
—Psalms 118:6 (NLT)

Scripture states no weapon formed against us will work (see **Isaiah 54:17**)!

The Lord is my light and my salvation; Whom shall I fear? The Lord is the defense of my life; Whom shall I dread?
—Psalms 27:1 (NASB)

Yes, this message has the power and potential to totally, transform your life. Sad to say many believers have been living below their true calling and destiny of God for their life. Scripture states in Christ Jesus, you are blessed with all spiritual blessings (see **Ephesians 1:3**).

VICTORY OVER AN ORPHAN SPIRIT

As this message of Sonship unfolds, it will drive away an orphan spirit that has been plaguing the Body of Christ. The wicked orphan spirit seeks to defame the Father's heart toward His children.

Many have been living a spiritual life as an impoverished person when in fact in Christ Jesus, you are spiritually rich beyond your wildest imagination. You are heir to the Kingdom of God. And Joint Heir with Christ the King.

51

Father God Predestined Us unto Sonship Through Jesus Christ

Shifting from Servant to Sonship

I want to emphasize that it is glorious and honorable to be a servant of the Most High God! I am in no way minimizing servanthood, yet there is much more. You are Heir to the Kingdom because you are a joint heir with Christ. It's time to move from servant to Sonship.

God's plans are always bigger and better than we could conceive for ourselves. God can do above and beyond anything we could ask or dare to think up!

Now to Him who is able to [carry out His purpose and] do superabundantly more than all that we dare ask or think [infinitely beyond our greatest prayers, hopes, or dreams], according to His power that is at work within us, to Him be the glory in the church and in Christ Jesus throughout all generations forever and ever. Amen.
—**Ephesians 3:20-21(AMPC)**

Open wide your spirit and drink deeply of these overwhelming promises and benefits of being a predestined son, a child of the King!

Blessed be the God and Father of our Lord Jesus Christ, who has blessed us with every spiritual blessing in the heavenly places in Christ, just as He chose us in Him before the foundation of the world,

that we would be holy and blameless before Him. In love He predestined us to adoption as sons through Jesus Christ to Himself, according to the kind intention of His will, to the praise of the glory of His grace, which He freely bestowed on us in the Beloved.
—Ephesians 1:3–6 (NASB)

This passage of scripture is overflowing with promises that are out of this world. Notice we have been blessed and favored with *every* spiritual blessing. We were chosen in Christ before the foundation of the world. We were predestined to be HIS son because of God's awesome love for us.

Let these promises flood and feed your soul:

—You are in Christ Jesus, blessed with every spiritual blessing!

—You were chosen by God before the foundation of the world to be holy and blameless!

—You are destined to be HIS son!

—You are called to purpose and power by God!

YOU HAVE DIVINE PURPOSE!

Don't let the devil steal your expectation! One of the saddest feelings in the world is the feeling that your life is going nowhere. Let this truth wash over your soul; you have been adopted into God's family, thru Christ, you are a son of God.

In Christ, you are destined to greatness! The Holy Spirit said to me *"tell the people of God except no imitation and then they can expect no limitation!"*

Never forget that in Christ you are an Heir to the Kingdom. In Christ and by Christ you can accomplish anything scripture states, you are equal to any task! You have been empowered by Christ!

I have strength for all things in Christ Who empowers me [I am ready for anything and equal to anything through Him Who infuses inner strength into me; I am self-sufficient in Christ's sufficiency].
—Philippians 4:13 (AMPC)

It is so important to be directed and guided by Holy Spirit; He alone can impart the wisdom and understanding to reveal our true stature with God.

For all who are allowing themselves to be led by the Spirit of God are sons of God. For you have not received a spirit of slavery leading again to fear [of God's judgment], but you have received the Spirit of adoption as sons [the Spirit producing sonship] by which we [joyfully] cry, "Abba! Father!"
—Romans 8:14 (AMPC)

Notice the protocol:

—We must be yielded and obedient to the guidance of Holy Spirit!

PART THREE: SONSHIP!

—We must understand our connection to God. He is our Father, and we are His sons.

The whole creation is crying out for us to move into our true destiny of *manifested sons of God*:

For the earnest expectation of the creation eagerly waits for the revealing of the sons of God.
—Romans 8:19 (NKJV)

Scripture states that The Spirit of Truth Himself reveals all creation is groaning and travailing, longing for and earnestly anticipating the revealing of true Divine Sonship.

For all who are led by the Spirit of God are sons of God. For [the Spirit which] you have now received [is] not a spirit of slavery to put you once more in bondage to fear, but you have received the Spirit of adoption [the Spirit producing sonship] in [the bliss of] which we cry, Abba (Father)! Father!

The Spirit Himself [thus] testifies together with our own spirit, [assuring us] that we are children of God.

And if we are [His] children, then we are [His] heirs also: heirs of God and fellow heirs with Christ [sharing His inheritance with Him]; only we must share His suffering if we are to share His glory. [But what of that?] For I consider that the sufferings of this present time (this present life) are not worth being compared with the glory that is about to be revealed to us and in us and for us and conferred on us!

For [even the whole] creation (all nature) waits expectantly and longs earnestly for God's sons to be made known [waits for the revealing, the disclosing of their sonship].

For the creation (nature) was subjected to frailty (to futility, condemned to frustration), not because of some intentional fault on its part, but by the will of Him Who so subjected it—[yet] with the hope

That nature (creation) itself will be set free from its bondage to decay and corruption [and gain an entrance] into the glorious freedom of God's children.

We know that the whole creation [of irrational creatures] has been moaning together in the pains of labor until now.

And not only the creation, but we ourselves too, who have and enjoy the firstfruits of the [Holy] Spirit [a foretaste of the blissful things to come] groan inwardly as we wait for the redemption of our bodies [from sensuality and the grave, which will reveal] our adoption (our manifestation as God's sons).

For in [this] hope we were saved. But hope [the object of] which is seen is not hope. For how can one hope for what he already sees?

PART THREE: SONSHIP!

But if we hope for what is still unseen by us, we wait for it with patience and composure.

—Romans 8:14-25 (AMPC)

In the realm of the Spirit, we are Kings and Priest, yet many are settling for living below the promises of Almighty God. It is time to shake off the dust of low esteem and step into your rightful inheritance.

And if you belong to Christ [if you are in Him], then you are Abraham's descendants, and [spiritual] heirs according to [God's] promise.

—Galatians 3:29 (AMP)

Within this passage is a wonderful key helping us to grasp the truth that all of God's promises belong to us; great benefit will be ours if we search out the promises of God, which are yes and amen to all who believe. We can and should claim every one of them.

And because you [really] are [His] sons, God has sent the Spirit of His Son into our hearts, crying out, "Abba! Father!"

Therefore you are no longer a slave (bond-servant), but a son; and if a son, then also an heir through [the gracious act of] God [through Christ].

—Galatians 4:6-7(AMPC)

HEIRS TO THE KINGDOM

Discovering the Season of Rings and Robes!

While waiting upon the Lord, I heard very clear within my spirit the Holy Spirit say; *"it's time for the ring and robe!"* The Father's heart is to bring us out of the pig pen of poor perception and into our inheritance because many have walked away from the Father's plan and are wasting away with an unfulfilled destiny.

It is time to come back to Father God; he has a RING and a ROBE for US!

And He said, There was a certain man who had two sons; And the younger of them said to his father, Father, give me the part of the property that falls [to me]. And he divided the estate between them.

And not many days after that, the younger son gathered up all that he had and journeyed into a distant country, and there he wasted his fortune in reckless and loose [from restraint] living.

And when he had spent all he had, a mighty famine came upon that country, and he began to fall behind and be in want.

So he went and forced (glued) himself upon one of the citizens of that country, who sent him into his fields to feed hogs.

PART THREE: SONSHIP!

And he would gladly have fed on and filled his belly with the carob pods that the hogs were eating, but [they could not satisfy his hunger and] nobody gave him anything [better].

Then when he came to himself, he said, How many hired servants of my father have enough food, and [even food] to spare, but I am perishing (dying) here of hunger!

I will get up and go to my father, and I will say to him, Father, I have sinned against heaven and in your sight.

I am no longer worthy to be called your son; [just] make me like one of your hired servants.

So he got up and came to his [own] father. But while he was still a long way off, his father saw him and was moved with pity and tenderness [for him]; and he ran and embraced him and kissed him [fervently].

And the son said to him, Father, I have sinned against heaven and in your sight; I am no longer worthy to be called your son [I no longer deserve to be recognized as a son of yours]!

But the father said to his bond servants, Bring quickly the best robe (the festive robe of honor) and put it on him; and give him a ring for his hand and sandals for his feet.

And bring out that [wheat-]fattened calf and kill it; and let us revel and feast and be happy and make merry,

Because this my son was dead and is alive again; he was lost and is found! And they began to revel and feast and make merry.
                              —Luke 15:11-24 (AMPC)

Another encouraging word that was spoken is: *"God said I am moving My people to deeper levels of maturity."* As we put our focus upon Christ the King, we are being transported to different dimensions of glory.

And all of us, as with unveiled face, [because we] continued to behold [in the Word of God] as in a mirror the glory of the Lord, are constantly being transfigured into His very own image in ever increasing splendor and from one degree of glory to another; [for this comes] from the Lord [Who is] the Spirit.
                              —2 Corinthians 3:18 (AMPC)

Christ is Heir of all things, and we are joint heirs with Him!

Scripture states that Our Lord Jesus Christ is heir to all things and we as His followers, are joint heirs with Him! We have equal to all that He has. Don't settle for less than your true inheritance.

PART THREE: SONSHIP!

And if [we are His] children, [then we are His] heirs also: heirs of God and fellow heirs with Christ [sharing His spiritual blessing and inheritance], if indeed we share in His suffering so that we may also share in His glory.
—Romans 8:17 (AMP)

Don't let the devil rob you another moment! It's time to take your stand and declare you are a joint heir with Christ the King. And in Him and by Him you are blessed with all spiritual blessings. From a heart of humility, stand strong in who you are in Christ.

Listen, my beloved brothers and sisters: has not God chosen the poor of this world to be rich in faith and [as believers to be] heirs of the kingdom which He promised to those who love Him?
—James 2:5 (AMP)

True wealth is to be rich in faith and heir to the kingdom of God. Our core goal is to seek first God's kingdom (see **Matthew 6:33**). When we are truly seeking first the will and way of God, we can be confident that God will put everything else in its proper place in our life (see **Proverbs 3:5-6**).

Scripture states that we are to walk in purity and power because of our true spiritual identity. We are not weak and worthless, on the contrary, we are "Sons and Daughters of Almighty God! Let's commit to living our true destiny.

Behold, what manner of love the Father hath bestowed upon us, that we should be called the sons of God: therefore the world knows us not, because it knew him not.

Beloved, now are we the sons of God, and it does not yet appear what we shall be: but we know that, when he shall appear, we shall be like him; for we shall see him as he is.

And every man that has his hope in him purify himself, even as he is pure.
—1 John 3:1-3 (KJV)

It is good and beneficial if we stop and take stock of our assets, not merely money and possessions but rather our position in Christ. Prayerfully study these passages which speak of the majesty, vastness, and immensity of Christ the King. Stop and reflect on your position. God's Word promises that you are now, at this present time, *a joint heir with Christ.*

This passage in Hebrews helps us to get a grasp of what is available to us.

[But] in the last of these days He has spoken to us in [the person of a] Son, Whom He appointed Heir and lawful Owner of all things, also by and through Whom He created the worlds and the reaches of space and the

ages of time [He made, produced, built, operated, and arranged them in order].

He is the sole expression of the glory of God [the Light-being, the out-raying or radiance of the divine], and He is the perfect imprint and very image of [God's] nature, upholding and maintaining and guiding and propelling the universe by His mighty word of power. When He had by offering Himself accomplished our cleansing of sins and riddance of guilt, He sat down at the right hand of the divine Majesty on high...

—Hebrews 1:2-3 (AMPC)

As we take time to ponder the greatness of Our Lord, let us be consumed with the vastness of His raging love for us.

Once in an angelic visitation and angel told me *"tell the Church at this point, they will learn more concerning the Majesty of the Master from the study of the book of Colossians than any book in the Bible!"*

Having said that; take time to study these verses from Colossians:

He is the exact living image [the essential manifestation] of the unseen God [the visible representation of the invisible], the firstborn [the preeminent one, the sovereign, and the originator] of all creation. For by Him all things were created in heaven and on earth, [things] visible and invisible, whether thrones or dominions or rulers or authorities; all things were created and exist through Him [that is, by His activity] and for Him. And He Himself existed and is before all things, and in Him all things hold together. [His is the controlling, cohesive force of the universe.] He is also the head [the life-source and leader] of the body, the church; and He is the beginning, the firstborn from the dead, so that He Himself will occupy the first place [He will stand supreme and be preeminent] in everything. For it pleased the Father for all the fullness [of deity—the sum total of His essence, all His perfection, powers, and attributes] to dwell [permanently] in Him (the Son), and through [the intervention of] the Son to reconcile all things to Himself, making peace [with believers] through the blood of His cross; through Him, [I say,] whether things on earth or things in heaven.

—Colossians 1:15-20 (AMP)

Some are confused concerning how to obtain their position as "sons of God. It is clear in Scripture this occurred the very moment you received and welcomed Christ into your heart as Lord and Savior.

But to as many as did receive and welcome Him, He gave the right [the authority, the privilege] to become children of God, that is, to those who believe in (adhere to, trust in, and rely on) His name—

—John 1:12 (AMP)

64

PART THREE: SONSHIP!

Christ Jesus in the sermon on the mount releases insights regarding being called the sons of God. We should be filled with joy, as we walk in God's favor expressing His character and functioning as peacemakers.

"Blessed [spiritually calm with life-joy in God's favor] are the makers and maintainers of peace, for they will [express His character and] be called the sons of God."
—Matthew 5:9 (AMP)

Scripture again, boldly states that if we are controlled and guided by the Spirit of God. We are indeed the sons of God!

For all who are led by the Spirit of God are sons of God.

For [the Spirit which] you have now received [is] not a spirit of slavery to put you once more in bondage to fear, but you have received the Spirit of adoption [the Spirit producing sonship] in [the bliss of] which we cry, Abba (Father)! Father!

The Spirit Himself [thus] testifies together with our own spirit, [assuring us] that we are children of God.
—Romans 8:14-16 (AMPC)

Notice this same passage in a different translation giving insights into the fact that we are joint heirs with Christ. We are not merely servants, but beloved sons.

SHEPHERD'S ROD 2018: SONSHIP!

For as many as are led by the Spirit of God, these are sons of God. For you did not receive the spirit of bondage again to fear, but you received the Spirit of adoption by whom we cry out, "Abba, Father." The Spirit Himself bears witness with our spirit that we are children of God, and if children, then heirs—heirs of God and joint heirs with Christ, if indeed we suffer with Him, that we may also be glorified together.
                    —Romans 8:14-17 (NKJV)

I've placed before you several other passages of Scripture that give reference to the fact that in Christ we are sons of God and thus, heirs to the Kingdom of God.

Please take time to grasp these biblical insights:

And it shall be that in the very place where it was said to them, You are not My people, they shall be called sons of the living God.
                    —Romans 9:26 (AMPC)

For in Christ Jesus you are all sons of God through faith.
                    —Galatians 3:26 (AMPC)

And because you [really] are [His] sons, God has sent the [Holy] Spirit of His Son into our hearts, crying, Abba (Father)! Father!
                    —Galatians 4:6 (AMPC)

That you may show yourselves to be blameless and guileless, innocent and uncontaminated, children of

PART THREE: SONSHIP!

God without blemish (faultless, unrebukable) in the midst of a crooked and wicked generation [spiritually perverted and perverse], among whom you are seen as bright lights (stars or beacons shining out clearly) in the [dark] world...

—Philippians 2:15 (AMPC)

Never forget you are the light of the world, a city set high on a hill giving light and life to a sin-darkened world (see **Matthew 5:14-16**). Arise and shine brighter and brighter (see **Isaiah 60:1-3**).

We are to be walking in victory, not as a defeated victim. In Christ, you are a super overcomer (see **Romans 8:37**)!

He who is victorious shall inherit all these things, and I will be God to him and he shall be My son.

—Revelation 21:7 (AMPC)

And if you belong to Christ [are in Him Who is Abraham's Seed], then you are Abraham's offspring and [spiritual] heirs according to promise.

—Galatians 3:29 (AMPC)

THE POISON OF POOR PERCEPTION

Saints must overcome spiritual stagnation and poor perceptions. The only real anti-venom for the poison of poor perception is the **truth** of God's Word. Only Truth

67

will reverse the effects of the venomous misconception concerning our actual identity (see **John 8:32**).

It's time we answer God's beckoning that we *Come Up Higher*!

MOVING FROM MILK TO STRONG MEAT

The Spirit of Truth spoke deep within in my spirit these compelling and challenging words: *"The remnant, the desperate hungry are moving to maturity, bring the Saints along!"* I asked Lord, how do I bring the sleeping sluggish Saints along? These words flooded my soul; ***"Awake and Arouse "Divine Hunger!"***

During these days, the saints of God must move in maturity, from milk to strong meat. Yes, we do need milk, but we must move into deeper insights of the Word of God (see **Hebrews 6:1**)

Like newborn infants, long for the pure spiritual milk, that by it you may grow up into salvation—
—1 Peter 2:2 (ESV)

We can't continue to remain on milk; we must develop and move onto deeper levels of the Word of God.

Notice this warning:

For though by this time you ought to be teachers, you need someone to teach you again the basic principles of

68

the oracles of God. You need milk, not solid food, for everyone who lives on milk is unskilled in the word of righteousness, since he is a child.

—Hebrews 5:12-13 (ESV)

We need strong motivation to flee from anything that seeks to distract and distance us from true intimacy with Christ.

Pay close attention to the warning and advice in the following passage:

So flee youthful passions and pursue righteousness, faith, love, and peace, along with those who call on the Lord from a pure heart.

—2 Timothy 2:22 (ESV)

True holiness must be in thoughts, words, and actions!

...For by your words you will be justified and acquitted, and by your words you will be condemned and sentenced.

—Matthew 12:35-37 (AMPC)

Paul admonishes us to get away fast from youthful lusts and anything that would defile our walk with Jesus.

Shun youthful lusts and flee from them, and aim at and pursue righteousness (all that is virtuous and good, right living, conformity to the will of God in thought, word, and deed); [and aim at and pursue] faith, love, [and] peace (harmony and concord with others) in

fellowship with all [Christians], who call upon the Lord out of a pure heart.
                    —2 Timothy 2:22 (AMPC)

We should put away childish ways and actions simply grow-up!

When I was a child, I spoke like a child, I thought like a child, I reasoned like a child. When I became a man, I gave up childish ways.
                    —1 Corinthians 13:11 (ESV)

The passage below speaks of our need to become much more informed by the Holy Scriptures. Saints need to move from milk to strong meat.

But strong meat belongeth to them that are of full age, even those who by reason of use have their senses exercised to discern both good and evil.
                    —Hebrews 5:14 (KJV)

The Spirit of Truth will assist the Saints of God to know their true identity. Yes! We are moving from *servants* to *Sons* this is both male and female. God is calling each of us to come higher and grow more and more like Christ. Never stop your quest to become more and more like the Master.

Therefore let us leave the elementary doctrine of Christ and go on to maturity, not laying again a foundation of repentance from dead works and of faith toward God, and of instruction about washings, the laying on of hands, the resurrection of the dead, and eternal judgment. And this we will do if God permits.

—Hebrews 6:1-3 (ESV)

Moving into Maturity

The goal and bar are set very high; our quest is to become more and more like Christ in every area of life. The mature measure is coming into the full stature of Christ. If this were not something obtainable, it would not be offered.

...until we all attain to the unity of the faith and of the knowledge of the Son of God, to mature manhood, to the measure of the stature of the fullness of Christ...

—Ephesians 4:13 (ESV)

Your Life Is Meaningful; You Have a Purposeful Future!

We were not created to live without a destiny (see **Ephesians 2:10**). We were made to be sustained by a meaningful, purposeful future (see **Jeremiah 31:17**).

God's Journal Directing Our Journey!

God, Himself has written down each of your days in His book (see **Psalms 139:15-16**). We need to harmonize

71

God's journal to our journey! This will truly be a life lived with divine purpose.

God's help is always here for us. We can be strengthened each day by this assurance, this confidence that: *what is happening in our lives today, no matter how mundane and ordinary, is a really significant step toward something good and great and beautiful, tomorrow.* Your spiritual tomorrow will not look like your today!

And we know that all things work together for good to those who love God, to those who are the called according to His purpose.

For whom He foreknew, He also predestined to be conformed to the image of His Son, that He might be the first born among many brethren. Moreover whom He predestined, these He also called; whom He called, these He also justified; and whom He justified, these He also glorified.

What then shall we say to these things? If God is for us, who can be against us? He who did not spare His own Son, but delivered Him up for us all, how shall He not with Him also freely give us all things? Who shall bring a charge against God's elect? It is God who justifies.

Who is he who condemns? It is Christ who died, and furthermore is also risen, who is even at the right hand

of God, who also makes intercession for us. Who shall separate us from the love of Christ? Shall tribulation, or distress, or persecution, or famine, or nakedness, or peril, or sword?
—Romans 8:28-35 (NKJV)

Remember weeping might last through the night but by God's bountiful favor, joy comes in the morning (see **Psalms 30:5**)! One single day can change your entire future. God's wonderful mercies are new every morning, great is God's love and faithfulness (see **Lamentations 3:21-23**).

"Destiny" and "Predestination"

These two words, *"destiny"* and *"predestination"* help to answer the tremendous cry of the human heart; *"is my life accomplishing anything?"* The word predestination speaks of Divine intent and purpose.

"God chose us in him before the foundation of the world."

"God predestined us to sonship through Jesus Christ for himself according to the good pleasure of his will." (see **Ephesians 1:4-5**)

God desires to establish in your hearts this fact that you are precious to Almighty God. You who believe in the Lord Jesus Christ and count him your Master and Savior and Lord—The Spirit of Truth wants to establish in your hearts an assured destiny, a great and beautiful future so that you don't ever have to moan over empty days.

For this is good and acceptable in the sight of God our Savior, who desires all men to be saved and to come to the knowledge of the truth.

—1 Timothy 2:3-4 (NKJV)

CHAPTER 4

DECLARE GOD'S GOODNESS AND KINDNESS!
Experience His Loving Kindness.

Bask in His Glory!

Psalm 118!

Each year the Lord highlights the Psalm that corresponds with the year. This year is 2018, as we dig deep into Psalm 118 we quickly discover this Psalm is a wonderful fountain, flowing with encouragement and soul-stirring inspiration. This Psalm starts and ends with a bold declaration directing us to express our adoration and high praise for Almighty God and all He has done for us.

Praise and adoration is the pathway to personal peace in one's life (see **Philippians 4:6-7**). When the dark clouds of doubt and despair attempt to set in, one of the most productive things you can do is maintain an attitude of gratitude, it will drive back the darkness and flood your soul with light and life.

Our *praise* has great transforming power to move the dark clouds of despair and depression away revealing the beaming rays of God's love.

We are clearly, instructed to give thanks, adoration, and praise to Almighty God our Heavenly Father for His everlasting mercy and loving-kindness. Never forget every good and perfect gift comes to us because of the Goodness of our Heavenly Father.

Every good thing given and every perfect gift is from above; it comes down from the Father of lights [the Creator and Sustainer of the heavens], in whom there is no variation [no rising or setting] or shadow cast by His turning [for He is perfect and never changes].
—James 1:17 (AMP)

Everything good and perfect that has entered our life is only because of the goodness of God. Your thirsty soul will be greatly refreshed and nourished; your spirit will soar as you take time to study and meditate upon each phrase of this Psalm. As we drink in these truths concerning God's overwhelming goodness and faithfulness to lavish His love upon us we are encouraged and inspired to stand strong, knowing we are not facing life alone. God will never forsake us (see **Hebrews 13:5**).

God delights in lavishing on us His wonderful mercies which are new each, and every morning (see **Lamentations**

PART FOUR: DECLARE GOD'S GOODNESS

3:22-23). Never doubt it Almighty God is good (see **Nahum 1:7**). God's plans are perfect and good; they are designed for our highest destiny (see **Jeremiah 29:11**).

This Psalm starts and ends with exhorting and encouraging everyone to bless and extol God for His wonderful mercies and loving kindness. The plan of God is to bless His people with ever-increasing favor (see **Psalms 84:11**). Moving us from one level of Glory to another.

Please take time to meditate upon each word of this Psalm; it is truly life-changing:

O give thanks to the Lord, for He is good; for His mercy and loving-kindness endure forever!

Let Israel now say that His mercy and loving-kindness endure forever.

Let the house of Aaron [the priesthood] now say that His mercy and loving-kindness endure forever.

Let those now who reverently and worshipfully fear the Lord say that His mercy and loving-kindness endure forever.

Out of my distress I called upon the Lord; the Lord answered me and set me free and in a large place.

The Lord is on my side; I will not fear. What can man do to me?

The Lord is on my side and takes my part, He is among those who help me; therefore shall I see my desire established upon those who hate me.

It is better to trust and take refuge in the Lord than to put confidence in man.

It is better to trust and take refuge in the Lord than to put confidence in princes.

All nations (the surrounding tribes) compassed me about, but in the name of the Lord I will cut them off!

They compassed me about, yes, they surrounded me on every side; but in the name of the Lord I will cut them off!

They swarmed about me like bees, they blaze up and are extinguished like a fire of thorns; in the name of the Lord I will cut them off!

You [my adversary] thrust sorely at me that I might fall, but the Lord helped me.

The Lord is my Strength and Song; and He has become my Salvation.

The voice of rejoicing and salvation is in the tents and private dwellings of the [uncompromisingly] righteous: the right hand of the Lord does valiantly and achieves strength!

PART FOUR: DECLARE GOD'S GOODNESS

The right hand of the Lord is exalted; the right hand of the Lord does valiantly and achieves strength!

I shall not die but live, and shall declare the works and recount the illustrious acts of the Lord.

The Lord has chastened me sorely, but He has not given me over to death.

Open to me the [temple] gates of righteousness; I will enter through them, and I will confess and praise the Lord.

This is the gate of the Lord; the [uncompromisingly] righteous shall enter through it.

I will confess, praise, and give thanks to You, for You have heard and answered me; and You have become my Salvation and Deliverer.

The stone which the builders rejected has become the chief cornerstone.

This is from the Lord and is His doing; it is marvelous in our eyes.

This is the day which the Lord has brought about; we will rejoice and be glad in it.

Save now, we beseech You, O Lord; send now prosperity, O Lord, we beseech You, and give to us success!

Blessed is he who comes in the name of the Lord; we bless you from the house of the Lord [you who come into His sanctuary under His guardianship].

The Lord is God, Who has shown and given us light [He has illuminated us with grace, freedom, and joy]. Decorate the festival with leafy boughs and bind the sacrifices to be offered with thick cords [all over the priest's court, right up] to the horns of the altar.

You are my God, and I will confess, praise, and give thanks to You; You are my God, I will extol You.

O give thanks to the Lord, for He is good; for His mercy and loving-kindness endure forever.

—Psalms 118 (AMPC)

I find it very helpful and beneficial to read the Scriptures in as many translations as I can find. I am fond of Eugene Peterson's The Message Bible; I like the way he uses common everyday language.

Please take time to read: **Psalm 118** in The Message translation:

Thank GOD because he's good, because his love never quits. Tell the world, Israel, "His love never quits." And you, clan of Aaron, tell the world, "His love never quits." And you who fear GOD, join in, "His love never quits."

PART FOUR: DECLARE GOD'S GOODNESS

Pushed to the wall, I called to GOD; from the wide open spaces, he answered. GOD's now at my side and I'm not afraid; who would dare lay a hand on me?

GOD's my strong champion; I flick off my enemies like flies. Far better to take refuge in GOD than trust in people; Far better to take refuge in GOD than trust in celebrities.

Hemmed in by barbarians, in GOD's name I rubbed their faces in the dirt; Hemmed in and with no way out, in GOD's name I rubbed their faces in the dirt; Like swarming bees, like wild prairie fire, they hemmed me in;

in GOD's name I rubbed their faces in the dirt. I was right on the cliff-edge, ready to fall, when GOD grabbed and held me.

GOD's my strength, he's also my song, and now he's my salvation. Hear the shouts, hear the triumph songs in the camp of the saved?

> *"The hand of GOD has turned the tide!*
> *The hand of GOD is raised in victory!*
> *The hand of GOD has turned the tide!"*
> *I didn't die. I lived!*

And now I'm telling the world what GOD did. GOD tested me, he pushed me hard, but he didn't hand me over to Death.

SHEPHERD'S ROD 2018: SONSHIP!

Swing wide the city gates—the righteous gates! I'll walk right through and thank GOD!

This Temple Gate belongs to GOD, so the victors can enter and praise.

Thank you for responding to me; you've truly become my salvation!

The stone the masons discarded as flawed is now the capstone!

This is God's work. We rub our eyes—we can hardly believe it! This is the very day God acted—let's celebrate and be festive!

Salvation now, God. Salvation now! Oh yes, God—a free and full life!

Blessed are you who enter in God's name—from God's house we bless you!

God is God, he has bathed us in light. Festoon the shrine with garlands, hang colored banners above the altar!

You're my God, and I thank you. O my God, I lift high your praise.

Thank God—he's so good.
His love never quits!

PART FOUR: DECLARE GOD'S GOODNESS

Some Points to Ponder:

Declare His Praise .... Psalm 118:1-4
All are invited to join this massive choir lifting our voices to extol Almighty God. Declaring His faithfulness and goodness and overflowing kindness which last forever. Let's join together to fill the earth with the highest praises for God!

Distress can Become the Doorway into God's Blessings Psalm118:5

God Is for US .... God Is on Our Side .... Psalm 118:6-7

Time to Trust:

*"It is better to trust in the L*ORD* Than to put confidence in man."*—Psalm 118:8 (NKJV)

In times of Weakness...Trust Him for Strength!

*Trust you in the L*ORD* for ever: for in the L*ORD* J*EHOVAH* is everlasting strength*—Isaiah 26:4 (KJV)

We all have periods of time when we feel somewhat weak and very vulnerable, this is the time when we need to trust God. When we are weak, He is strong. He is truly our strong tower and our strong, sure stable Rock.

The apostle Paul wrote that when he was at his weakest point, that is when he was strongest...because then he trusted the Lord to get him through.

"And he said unto me, My grace is sufficient for thee: for my strength is made perfect in weakness. Most gladly therefore will I rather glory in my infirmities, that the power of Christ may rest upon me."
—2 Corinthians 12:9 (KJV)

Hold on to this wonderful promise of God as he states: *"My grace is sufficient for you!"*

God's Presence Eradicates Fear!

Fear not, for I am with you; Be not dismayed, for I am your God. I will strengthen you, Yes, I will help you, I will uphold you with My righteous right hand.'
—Isaiah 41:10 (NKJV)

In times when we are Unsure of Our Way... Trust Him for Direction!

Trust in the Lord, and do good; so shalt thou dwell in the land, and verily thou shalt be fed.

Delight thyself also in the Lord: and he shall give thee the desires of thine heart.

Commit thy way unto the Lord; trust also in him; and he shall bring it to pass.
—Psalm 37:3-5 (KJV)

84

PART FOUR: DECLARE GOD'S GOODNESS

Trust in the LORD with all thine heart; and lean not unto thine own understanding. In all thy ways acknowledge him, and he shall direct thy paths.
                                                    —Proverbs 3:5-6

When it seems darkest, that is when we should trust Him!

Thy word is a lamp unto my feet, and a light unto my path.
                                              —Psalm 119:105 (KJV)

In Times When We Don't Understand...Trust His Loving Care!

Trust in the LORD with all thine heart; and lean not unto thine own understanding.
                                               —Proverbs 3:5 (KJV)

Trust in the fact that God is always working things for our good, even when we can't see it in the present. Nevertheless, God promises He is working for our good.

And we know that all things work together for good to them that love God, to them who are the called according to his purpose.
                                              —Romans 8:28 (KJV)

Job in the midst of desperate times states he will trust in God's goodness:

Though he slay me, yet will I trust in him: but I will maintain mine own ways before him.
—Job 13:15 (KJV)

When is it time to Trust the Lord?

- In times of Weakness...Trust Him for Strength!

- In Times When We Are Unsure of Our Way...Trust Him for Direction!

- In Times When We Don't Understand ...Trust His Loving Care

- Trust in Him all of the time!

Trust in him at all times; ye people, pour out your heart before him: God is a refuge for us. Selah.
—Psalm 62:8 (KJV)

Behold, God is my salvation; I will trust, and not be afraid: for the LORD JEHOVAH is my strength and my song; he also is become my salvation.
—Isaiah 12:2 (KJV)

PART FOUR: DECLARE GOD'S GOODNESS

Beloved, let these promises build confidence and give you courage within your heart and soul.

*Say this out loud –"**THE LORD IS ON MY SIDE;***

I WILL NOT FEAR!"

CHAPTER 5

PROPHETIC EVENTS
Prophetic Perspectives and Revelatory Insights.

Watchman! Watchman! What Do You See?

I will convey the events and encounters that began to unfold and share some of the revelatory insights which I received on the Day of Atonement. I received these revelations by dreams, visions, trances as well as a visitation. My heart's deepest desire is I want God to communicate to me in any manner He would choose. My heart cries: *speak LORD your servant is listening.*

You should, of course, seek the Lord and ask Him to reveal the deeper meaning of these revelations to you. One thing I want to do is to stir and stimulate you to seek God for revelation and interpretation for yourself. Scripture states we are to write the vision (revelations) and make it clear so the people can clearly, grasp it and move with it. I am following the instructions given to me by God from this passage.

SHEPHERD'S ROD 2018: SONSHIP!

*"This is what the L*ORD *God of Israel says: Write in a book everything that I tell you."*
—Jeremiah 30:2 (GW)

The Prophet Habakkuk reveals some keen insights on receiving and recording revelation. He states; I will stand upon my watch to see and observe what God is doing and saying.

And the Lord answered me and said, Write the vision and engrave it so plainly upon tablets that everyone who passes may [be able to] read [it easily and quickly] as he hastens by.
—Habakkuk 2:2 (AMPC)

I will not attempt to cover these events in their totality; I want you to dig deeper into them. If you prayerfully seek God for deeper revelation regarding these events, you can expect great benefit to come to your spiritual life

This year like years before God would begin to pull back the veil to reveal the coming revelations. It's like beholding lightening in the night sky, you can see it many miles away, but it takes some time for the sound of the rumble of the thunder to arrive. It is very difficult to convey heavenly experiences with human words. We must depend upon the Holy Spirit to reveal these truths to the heart.

Scripture states that our natural mind can't correctly comprehend the things of the Spirit they (the revelations and visitations) must be spiritually discerned.

PART FIVE: PROPHETIC EVENTS

These things we also speak, not in words which man's wisdom teaches but which the Holy Spirit teaches, comparing spiritual things with spiritual. But the natural man does not receive the things of the Spirit of God, for they are foolishness to him; nor can he know them, because they are spiritually discerned. But he who is spiritual judges all things, yet he himself is rightly judged by no one. For "who has known the mind of the LORD that he may instruct Him?" But we have the mind of Christ
—1 Corinthians 6:13-15 (NKJV)

Treasures of The Deep

The very instant I laid my head on my pillow, suddenly, I was catapulted into an encounter. I am no longer in my bed, now I am in a pure white room, so white and brilliant that the entire room is radiant with light. Alone and somewhat stunned, I am standing there wondering where I am and what I am doing here. Suddenly a man appears mere inches in front of me.

His appearance startled me; his hair was a strangely beautiful silver grey, it almost touched his shoulders, his face was handsome and pleasant, his skin was smooth with a golden tone. He seemed to be someone I knew, but I was not sure, so I asked him his name, and he said in a joyful tone, with a huge smile on his face "my name is Lloyd Bridges." However, I knew he was truly a messenger angel.

The name Lloyd speaks of grey hair which speaks of *divine wisdom*. And the last name Bridges speaks of making access between two places, something that connects speaks of links and passages.

Another aspect is that there was an actor that starred in a television series from 1958-1961 titled Sea Hunt.

I inquired asking the messenger, "What am I doing here?" He quickly replied, "I am here to help you prepare to go into the deep to retrieve the hidden treasure."

And with a touch of his hand in a split-second, I am dressed in a huge underwater deep-sea diving suit. It had a huge helmet which seemed to be constructed out of silver, equipped with a bluish face glass to see out. I ask Lloyd "why am I going into the deep water," he said with a huge smile "you are going after the hidden treasures of the deep!"

As he was placing the silver helmet up on my head, he said in an instructive tone, "You will go deep into the water of the Word, because deep is calling to deep!"

The next step in this encounter, I am in the deep sea. It seemed if I was miles underwater. However, it was dim and dark. I could clearly, hear his words of instruction: "simply extend your right hand," to which I did, and at that moment a very strong bright light began to flow from my hand. The light settled on the entrance to a huge underwater cave. I was instructed to enter into the huge underwater cave. To my total surprise, I see about a dozen very old men dressed in robes like the High Priest would have worn in Bible times. However, these robes were beautiful beyond words, they were golden brownish and shimmering green with silver and gold threads woven into the fabric. Their robes were like nothing I had ever seen. Somehow it appeared that their robes were empowering them to be mobile and giving them the ability to move about.

I noticed they were not in underwater diving equipment, they were walking and talking like normal. Additionally, I realized these men were not in water at all they were totally dry. One of the men spoke concerning the deep diving equipment; I was wearing saying, "you can take that off, you are in a different environment, the atmosphere here is ratified wholesome air." Ratified carries with it the meaning of sanctioned, endorsed, authorized and confirmed.

Each of these men had in their hand's scrolls; you could sense the value they put upon these written scrolls. To them, they were most precious.

I questioned asking; "what are these scrolls and what is written upon them?" One of the men looked deep into my eyes and slowly pulled open the tip of the scroll. Within his hand, he exposed only these words: ***The secret things belong unto the LORD our GOD but those things which are revealed belong unto us and to our descendants forever, that we may do all the works of the book"*** **—Deuteronomy 29:29**.

I said; "yes I know this passage, but what is written on your scrolls?" To which in perfect unison all of the men boldly spoke: *"the road to reformation!"* We have been waiting to release them! The Church stands in need of reformation that will bring about radical revival. The demise of true reformation is a spirit of contentment and compromise. There must come a desperation for the presence and power of God. These hidden treasures will begin to release a divine hunger to know God on much deeper levels.

And I will give you the treasures of darkness and hidden riches of secret places, that you may know that it is I, the Lord, the God of Israel, Who calls you by your name.
—Isaiah 45:3 (AMPC)

Hope Is Growing Brighter!

As I look about my surroundings, my attention was directed to leaves moving about on the tops of huge trees. I heard a wonderful message blowing in the soft breeze. The Spirit spoke and said, *"listen with your heart,"* and within my spirit, I clearly, heard these words: **"Hope is growing brighter!"**

Yes! Hope is growing brighter and brighter for the people who choose to walk in the pathway of Truth and Light (see **Psalms 36:9**)!

For all who put their trust and confidence in God and His Word their soul will be strong. Courage will spring forth, giving evidence of victory over all adversity, knowing by our actions that we are more than conquers (see **Romans 8:37**).

The righteous will be bold as a lion (see **Proverbs 28:1**). Many will be greatly refreshed from fresh wellsprings of hope (see **Proverbs 13:12**). Guard your heart don't let anything stop the wellspring of life from flowing brighter and brighter (see **Proverbs 4:23**). Hold on tight to hope (see **Hebrews 10:35**).

America will begin to Repent!

In a short vision, I was shown the stars on the American Flag began to twinkle, and then began to shine much brighter. A fresh wave of God's presence will move within our nation. Our nation will cry-out in repentance. From the repentance, will come healing and restoring.

The grassroots people are standing up and standing out. It is high time for people to get back to common sense and doing the right thing! Enough of these so-called political protests which are mostly paid crooks, looking to loot and riot.

Expect to see huge strides of growth in American jobs and employment.

There will be a reaping sickle thrust into the lawless government in Washington DC! Crooked corrupt political leaders will be cut down; some will face strong criminal charges. The swamp will begin to drain in a much swifter manner.

The cry, one nation under God, will again be heard. Prayers will be heard in the halls of Congress and the government will be a friend to the Body of Christ.

There will be ministry sessions within the walls of government buildings. Much greater wisdom will be released.

PRAY FOR EUROPE

Please intercede for Europe!

Dark, Dangerous Days for much of Europe – Radical Islamic Jihadist must be restrained. For years, because of uncontrolled borders, they have infiltrated and permeated much of Europe. Let us pray that these evil cells will be exposed and eliminated before they can finish their diabolical plots. These are plots and plans for demons of death and destruction; they must be bound and cast down.

These radical Islamic Jihadist are brutal, barbaric murders and are moving swiftly into Southeast Asia, the Philippines, Indonesia, Malaysia and much of Africa. These demons know no bounds concerning ethnicity. Never forget this is a spiritual battle manifesting in the natural realm.

PART FIVE: PROPHETIC EVENTS

The Devils Plan is for Wars to erupt and explode in nations around the world. However, God's plans are for peace!

Let's join with Christ in His prayer: *"Thy Kingdom come Thy will be done on earth as it is in heaven!"*

TICKING TIME BOMB —NORTH KOREA (2005)

I received this revelation on the Day of Atonement 2004. This word given in the Shepherd's Rod Volume X Titled: The Belt of Truth in **2005** is so important to hear and heed **today**!

TICKING TIME BOMB — NORTH KOREA (2018)

This warning was released on page 138 of the 2005 Shepherd's Rod Volume X.

I was shown that North Korea was a real threat and a ticking time bomb. However, the Church can and must defuse this bomb with intercessory prayer. It is time to rise up and drive back the spirit of death and destruction. *True intercessor prayer can and must stop this ticking clock.* Do you see how important it is to take very seriously the prophetic warnings?

I strongly and urgently warned about this deadly threat in 2002 now all these years have come and gone, and the threat is very real today.

THE THREE-TOED — DRAGON

I've very rarely spoken of this subject openly! Several years ago, I was summoned into the Courts of Heaven. I was instructed to go into South Korea and do spiritual warfare to drive back a three-toed dragon that was poised to come out of a cave and start World War Three! I did go and was obedient to the commission I had been assigned. It was a success; the three-toed dragon had been driven back. However, now it has reappeared at the mouth of the cave eager to start a nuclear war. Please join me as we arise taking our God-given authority and drive back this wicked event (see **Matthew 18:18**).

Join in the army of Saints that are praying for God's protection and direction during these dangerous dark days.

Mainstream Media

The only way to correctly describe and discern what is taking place with many in the mainstream media in the United States of America is it is demonic, not merely mean, but is devilish! Much of the news media is at this point, a very effective tool in the hands of the devil, helping to spread discord and division which is without a doubt fostered by the devil.

The mainstream media in the United States has done more to dismantle America than all the outside attacks. The propaganda they spread is poisonous. The media are guilty of spearheading division, discontentment, and chaos in our nation. The Bible informs us about those who plant "*Seeds "of Discord* and *"Sowers of Discord!"*

A heart that manufactures wicked thoughts and plans, feet that are swift in running to evil,

A false witness who breathes out lies [even under oath], and he who sows discord among his brethren.
—Proverbs 6:18-19 (AMPC)

The news outlets are guilty of sowing the seeds of bitterness, anger, rebellion, distrust, and hatred into the soil of other people's hearts and souls. These actions do *not come from the Spirit of God*. Such divisive behavior is included in what the Bible calls *"the works of the flesh."*

Now the doings (practices) of the flesh are clear (obvious): they are immorality, impurity, indecency, Idolatry, sorcery, enmity, strife, jealousy, anger (ill temper), selfishness, divisions (dissensions), party spirit (factions, sects with peculiar opinions, heresies),

Envy, drunkenness, carousing, and the like. I warn you beforehand, just as I did previously, that those who do such things shall not inherit the kingdom of God.
—Galatians 5:19-21 (AMPC)

Understand this is not a fleshly battle but a spiritual one. It is not '*this man versus that man*' but '*the spiritual enemies of Christ versus His Kingdom.*'

For we wrestle not against flesh and blood, but against principalities, against powers, against the rulers of the darkness of this world, against spiritual wickedness in high places.
            —Ephesians 6:12 (KJV)

The mainstream media should be tried for treason! The definition of treason: *is the attempted overthrow of a setting government.* They are guilty of continued attempts to cause confusion and bring about a coup. One of the only ways to silence them is to stop patronizing their sponsors, **don't buy what they are selling**.

Another Warning!
Arising Culture of Anarchy.... Lawlessness on Levels not seen!

Antifa is a wicked movement, now in America and their numbers are growing. Their goal is to *overthrow* America! These are not simply misguided young people. No, this is a very violent, wicked movement with its roots deep in Marxism. Most of the so-called protesters are nothing but paid anarchist; their goal is to dismantle and destroy America as we have known it. One of the things we as followers of Christ can do is to become much **bolder** in our *stand for Christ and His Kingdom*. We are to be a bright light a city on a hill sending forth the light of God's grace and love.

PART FIVE: PROPHETIC EVENTS

What is going on with all these Earthquakes, Hurricanes, Floods, Raging Wild Fires, Volcanic Activity, Tornadoes, on and on?

Worldwide, I get questions about what is going on with all the natural disasters? The cry of many in the world today is; what is going on with all the displays of nature and why is this taking place? It is the role and responsibility of the Prophet to help answer questions like these.

Here are some of the answers to these many questions:

All OF CREATION IS CRYING OUT!
From ABOVE and BELOW!

All of Creation Is Crying Out! Longing for Saints to step into their true destiny (see **Romans 8:19**)! The Earth will shake, and rivers of fire will flow, as the depths of the Earth are swelling. All Creation is in travail or birthing pains!

These birth pains are manifested in earthquakes and mighty mountains are erupting, spewing ash and rivers of fire across the lands. Storms over water are more frequent and fierce than any time in recorded history. We see this manifested in strong winds, heavy rains and huge waves.

Worldwide major volcanic and seismic disturbances on levels not seen in our time. The center of the earth is quickly expanding. The mountains will blow, and the rivers of fire will flow. Expect to see ash in the air and rivers of burning lava flowing. We will see seismic earthquakes and volcanic activity at an all-time high. As the Earth shutters, the bowels of the Earth are convulsing.

Expect to see more earthquakes than ever in the history of the earth. Rocks will tumble and rumble down. Waves will roar, and winds will rush. Truly the mountains and rocks will cry out

The creation is crying out for Sons and Daughters to move into maturity.

Winds will respond in a fashion not seen in our time. The waves of the seas will roar, and jet streams in the air will soar. Turbulence will be in the air in a different dimension than before; this is the natural exposing the supernatural.

SIGNS IN THE HEAVENS

Creation will begin to speak loudly; the heavens will put on a light show unseen in our day. We will hear announcements of distant discoveries of stars and planets not known until now. All of these speak of the coming heavenly revelation that will be revealed in our day.

Great Turbulence in the Heavens!

PART FIVE: PROPHETIC EVENTS

THE STARS ABOVE — Asteroids and Angels!

There will be light shows in the Heavens.

So-called Northern Lights Will Demonstrate and Display Like never before.
Meteor Showers!

We will behold meteoroids and meteors on a scale not seen in our lifetime. Comets will be coming and going; their orbits will be extremely erratic; this will be a sign in the heavens speaking of angelic activity. The Hosts of heaven, both holy and hellish will be active, speaking of angels and demons…there will be reports of objects in the heavens that have never been seen before. The curtains are being pulled back; truly these are the days of "revelations"!

Fool's Gold…. Don't Except the Fake!

While waiting before the Lord, within my spirit, I heard the Spirit of Truth declare… "I am exposing pyrite!" Not sure what the Lord was communicating, I said: "please explain this to me." He said; "it is fool's gold, it has the appearance of real gold. However, it is worthless." He said to me; "do not permit or tolerate My people settling for pyrite (fool's gold) when they can have the real glory.

Pyrite: The mineral pyrite, also known as fool's gold, is an iron sulfide with the chemical formula FeS_2. **Pyrite** is considered the most common of the sulfide minerals. **Pyrite's** metallic luster and pale brass-yellow hue give it a superficial resemblance to gold, hence the well-known nickname of fool's gold.

It is a tragedy how many people are deceived into thinking they have something valuable and worthwhile, yet it is worthless fool's gold. How can we identify the fake and false from the real and genuine? Here is a test:

For no other foundation can anyone lay than that which is [already] laid, which is Jesus Christ (the Messiah, the Anointed One).

But if anyone builds upon the Foundation, whether it be with gold, silver, precious stones, wood, hay, straw,

The work of each [one] will become [plainly, openly] known (shown for what it is); for the day [of Christ] will disclose and declare it, because it will be revealed with fire, and the fire will test and critically appraise the character and worth of the work each person has done.
—1 Corinthians 3:11-13 (AMPC)

A Time of Revealing!

A time of uncovering what evil people have been concealing…. this is time to come clean. Those covering their sins will not prosper.

He who covers his transgressions will not prosper, but whoever confesses and forsakes his sins will obtain mercy.
— Proverbs 28:13 (AMPC)

104

PART FIVE: PROPHETIC EVENTS

HEALING ANOINTING

The healing anointing will significantly increase! A wonderful fresh wave of healing anointing will come upon the Saints. Prayer lines will form on city streets for healings and deliverances. The Lord is releasing an awesome anointing for healing and deliverance (see **Isaiah 61:1**). Many will operate in the pattern of Christ Jesus (see **Matthew 4:23**).

The Color This Year Is Purple - *Purple is a royal color*

I was told look up into the heavens, lifting my natural eyes to the heavens, I saw the heavens were filled with beautiful, outstanding clouds but not like any clouds I had seen before they were purple in color.

I questioned; "Lord what are the purple clouds?" to which He replied, "you are seeing the royal robes of the Saints." He continued saying "many are coming into their royal priesthood, they are grasping the truth of **Revelation 1:5-6**."

Purple is mentioned fifty-three times in Scripture, and so it must obviously play a prominent role in the Bible. Purple is a color that shows wealth, royalty, and status. Purple was often a color that was very expensive and difficult to make and manufacture. As such, royalty would often be seen wearing it.

105

Purple is a mixture of blue and red. Blue speaks of revelation and red speaks of redemption. Purple is very important in the accessories in the ancient temples of Israel, including the curtain of the tabernacle, the veil of the tabernacle, the ephod of the high priest, the girdle that the high priest wore, the breastplate of the high priest and even the hem of the priests' robe. Purple is even the color covering the brazen altar, so we know from history, both biblical and secular history, that purple is the color most often associated with royalty.

In addition to Jesus clothed in a color (purple) that denotes royalty, other verses further the fact that purple is seen as a symbol of royalty in the Bible. For instance, **Proverbs 31:22** says of the virtuous woman: *"she makes tapestry for herself; her clothing is fine linen and purple."* In other words, she has a good quality fabric that she makes, all because she works hard and is very skilled at what she does.

Interestingly, there was another woman who did something similar, but this time in the New Testament. **Acts 16:14** states: *"One who heard us was a woman named Lydia, from the city of Thyatira, a seller of purple goods, who was a worshiper of God. The Lord opened her heart to pay attention to what was said by Paul."* So, there was yet another indication in the Bible that the color purple was a very, expensive and wealthy color to make and have.

PART FIVE: PROPHETIC EVENTS

Cyber Wars Will Escalate!

We will be shocked to discover how unstable the cyber world really is. As technology continues to accelerate at a blinding speed, we will see more important data being attacked and erased. Suddenly more and more cybercrimes will be reported. These attacks will include taking our information hostage for ransom.

GOOD NEWS CONCERNING THE GOODNESS OF THE GOSPEL!
Evangelism WILL EXPLODE!!!

The Main Thing!

Evangelism WILL EXPLODE!!! Souls! Souls! Souls! And more souls.

- THE WORKERS ARE WILLING AND WINSOME!
- THE MAIN THING WILL BE THE MAIN THING — *"WINNING SOULS!"*
- THE HARVESTERS WILL RUSH INTO THE FIELDS, AND GREAT WILL BE THE HARVEST OF SOULS — *EXPECT MUCH FRUIT!*

FALSE GODS WILL BE POOR PROTECTION FOR THE SPIRIT OF DEATH AND DESTRUCTION!

Much death and destruction will occur where nations worship false gods. They will find out their gods will not

107

answer nor aid them in their cries for help. Only *our God* is gracious and merciful.

Many will be delivered from false religions. Because the people cried out to empty and false gods, they had no help. But Almighty God, in tender mercy, will reveal HIMSELF!

THE GOSPEL LIGHT WILL BE BRIGHT IN DARK PLACES.

PRAY FOR the peace of Israel! The foe will attempt to excise political power against Israel but to no avail. However, Iran will soon have constructed a nuclear warhead and Israel will take preemptive measures.

Let This Be Your Moto — *God's Plans are for MY BEST!*

For I know the thoughts and plans that I have for you, says the Lord, thoughts and plans for welfare and peace and not for evil, to give you hope in your final outcome.
—Jeremiah 29:11 (AMPC)

GET TO KNOW AND ACQUAINT YOURSELF WITH GOD!

Acquaint now yourself with Him [agree with God and show yourself to be conformed to His will] and be at peace; by that [you shall prosper and great] good shall come to you—Job 22:21 (AMPC).

Learn from the Sunflower

We must keep our face and focus upon the Son just as the sunflower keeps its face following the sun. We too will grow and bear fruit when we stay focused on beholding the Son's face. We will become what we behold —**face to face** —His face changes our face!

The Centricity of Christ

A radical return to preaching and sharing the simple, profound gospel!

With great response, people will welcome the preaching of the good news! Expect to see many souls coming to Christ the King.

Change is in the Air

I saw coins from all different nations falling from the sky to the ground; I said: "Lord, what does this mean?" to which deep within my spirit I heard "change is taking place all over the world." The winds of change are blowing stronger! The wise will began to pick up the pieces.

IT IS A SHAKE-UP TO PRODUCE A WAKE-UP!

All about our world we see earthquakes, floods, eruptions of mountains, falling rocks and the opening of sinkholes swallowing entire homes. What is going on in the natural is a picture of what is going on in the spiritual realm. God is shaking things to get our attention back to Him.

At that time his voice shook the earth, but now he has promised, "Once more I will shake not only the earth but also the heavens." The words "once more" indicate the removing of what can be shaken—that is, created things—so that what cannot be shaken may remain.
—Hebrews 12:26-27 (NIV)

God will shake everything that can be shaken in our life until all that remains is of Him. Much like a strong wind that blows the dead leaves from a tree, God will blow away all the unnecessary distractions that have nested in the branches of our life.

GOD IS FOR US NOT AGAINST US!

God longs to help us not to hurt us. He often pulls us out of our comfort zones so that we can grow deeper in Him. Sometimes we go through a cold winter so that our roots will go down deep to our Source; other times we enjoy a spring season of abundant rain. No matter what season we are in, God is always there with us (see **Nahum 1:7**). It brings such courage and confidence knowing that Father God's plans and purposes for us are for good. He delights to display His overwhelming goodness in our lives. May we be ambassadors of joy and gladness beaming out God's love and light in a world filled with despair.

PART FIVE: PROPHETIC EVENTS

The Purpose of the Process

Do not miss the purpose of the process. God does not shake you to torment you. He shakes you to awaken you. The pruning of the tree is not to kill the tree but to aid the tree in bearing better fruit; this is God's process in our life.

The Time of Sifting and Shaking Is Upon Us

The sifting and shaking will continue to accelerate as He separates the sheep from the goats. Everything that can be shaken will be shaken. What is coming will separate the real from the counterfeit. Lives built on the shifting sands of secular, worldly wisdom will surely fail and fall. However, for all who have built upon the ROCK and the wisdom of the written Word, which is the Living Word Christ, their house will stand strong (see **Matthew 7:24-27**).

Faulty Foundation

If you are receiving your affirmation, love, self-worth, joy, strength, or acceptance from any source other than God, He will shake it. He does not do this to cause you pain; rather, He wants to pull you closer to Himself. Make sure you don't try, in your strength to rebuild what God has shaken in your life. He desires to rebuild everything in you so that your only life source is in Him.

It is time to face the facts...what is God trying to shake in our life? It is time we submit to God's truth so that we can experience His true freedom. Even though God might be shaking us, yet from that, He is giving us an unshakeable kingdom!

"Therefore, since we are receiving a kingdom that cannot be shaken, let us be thankful, and so worship God acceptably with reverence and awe, for our "God is a consuming fire."
—Hebrews 12:28-29 (NIV)

FIRM FOUNDATIONS that can't be shaken!

It is especially encouraging that in a world of change and decay there are some things which can never be shaken. In **Hebrews 12:28-29**, we discover that a time of shaking is to be expected, for the writer predicts that there is coming a dreadful, terrible time in the world when everything, except certain things which can never be shaken, will be dissolved and removed (see **2 Peter 3:10**).

Today, in our world, a great shaking is going on, and in connection with this, we should recall Jesus' parable recorded in **Matthew 7:24-29**. All that is not built upon the Rock will fall, and only things of eternal value will stand.

Globally, there is chaos and collapse on an unprecedented scale; our culture because of compromise seems to be shaken to the core.

PART FIVE: PROPHETIC EVENTS

Praise the Lord Jesus, there is another side to the story, for there are some things which can never be shaken! We are seeing God's people take a strong stand for uprightness and holiness. I am so encouraged to see leadership taking a bold stance for truth (see **Proverbs 23:23**). It is only the pure Truth of God's Word that will prepare us for service (see **John 17:17**)!

THE WORD OF GOD CAN NEVER BE SHAKEN!

Be assured of this, the Word of God is correct:

Heaven and earth will perish and pass away, but My words will not perish or pass away.
—Mark 13:31 (AMPC)

You have been regenerated (born again), not from a mortal origin (seed, sperm), but from one that is immortal by the ever living and lasting Word of God. For all flesh (mankind) is like grass, and all its glory (honor) like [the] flower of grass. The grass withers and the flower drops off,

But the Word of the Lord (divine instruction, the Gospel) endures forever. And this Word is the good news which was preached to you.
—1 Peter 1:23-25 (AMPC)

THE BIBLE'S PROMISES CAN NEVER BE SHAKEN!

It has been estimated that there are 30,000 promises, yet not one has ever failed or will ever fail. There are promises for every child of God, for every situation in life. These promises become ours when we put our faith in the Lord Jesus Christ.

Whatever God has promised gets stamped with the Yes of Jesus. In him, this is what we preach and pray, the great Amen, God's Yes and our Yes together, gloriously evident. God affirms us, making us a sure thing in Christ, putting his Yes within us. By his Spirit he has stamped us with his eternal pledge—a sure beginning of what he is destined to complete.
—2 Corinthians 1:20 (MSG)

THE BIBLE'S POWER AND AUTHORITY CAN NEVER BE SHAKEN!

The Word of God has power:

—Of Assurance! Romans 1:16 and Hebrews 4:12

—To Convict! Acts 2:37

—To Convert! Psalm 19:7

—To Cleanse! Psalm 119:9

—To Comfort! Psalm 119:49-50

—To Counsel! Psalm 73:24

And the power of God's Word will never change.

PART FIVE: PROPHETIC EVENTS

THE BIBLE'S PROPHECIES CAN NEVER BE SHAKEN!

Many in society today may scoff at the prophecies contained in the Bible, but by doing so, they only fulfill the Bible (see **2 Peter 3:3-4**).

Many of the Bible's prophecies have already been literally fulfilled, and all the promises that await fulfillment will also be literally fulfilled.

Thank God that in a shaking and unstable world our chart and compass are secure!

The Word of God, the Bible, is thoroughly reliable and unfailing:

- If it is a convicting Word, have I been *convicted*?
- If it is a converting Word, have I been *converted*?
- If it is a cleansing Word, am I being *cleansed*?
- If it is a comforting Word, do I receive its *comfort*?
- If it is a counseling Word, do I act upon its *wisdom*?

THE THRONE OF GOD CAN NEVER BE SHAKEN!

When we turn to **Psalm 45:6** and **Lamentations 5:19** we can lift up our hearts with gratitude that whatever else may happen, God's throne will remain secure.

115

SHEPHERD'S ROD 2018: SONSHIP!

Today, we have to look above our sense of time to find things that are permanent, look up **Psalm 90:12** and compare with **Psalm 46:1-5 and 7**.

Even the heavens will be shaken one day — look up **Isaiah 34:4**; but God, who is above the heavens, is eternal and immutable. Nothing can shake or change Him (see **Hebrews 1:10-12**). It must be a great encouragement to every child of God to know that when everything else is shaken, *the throne of God can never be shaken.*

We must, of course, reckon with God's throne. As it is a throne of grace (see **Hebrews 4:16**) and it is also a throne of judgment (see **Revelation 20:11**). Are you a subject of the King who sits upon the throne of heaven (see **Colossians 1:13**)?

THE CHURCH OF GOD CAN NEVER BE SHAKEN!

The words of our Lord recorded in **Matthew 16:18** assure us of this. In this amazing statement, the Savior was assuring His disciples (and us) that the Church is built on the solid foundation of His person and His work. There is no other foundation (see **1 Corinthians 3:11**).

Today churches and man-made organized assemblies or communities of professing Christians are being shaken in every way; but the Church, which is the Body of Christ, cannot and will not be shaken. The true Church is secure, permanent and abiding. There is a great difference between being a Church member and a Christian. Are you a member of the true Church? That is, not only a professing Christian but a possessing Christian?

THE CHILD OF GOD CAN NEVER BE SHAKEN!

Many biblical promises assure us of God's concern for every one of His children and of His pledge to keep them secure until they are safely ''home'' with Him in heaven.

For example, look up the following verses:

> **John 10:27-29**
> **Romans 8:38-39**
> **1 John 2:17**
> **2 Timothy 1:12**

You are a child of God! You have been born into His family!

Also, look up these verses:

> **John 1:12**
> **John 3:5**
> **1 John 3:10**

Let every Christian rejoice that in a shaking world these things can never be shaken. Do you belong to the

Lord? Are you a subject in His kingdom and living in subjection to His Word? Are you a child of God through faith in Jesus Christ?

CONCLUSION

The Choice Is Yours
Live at the Highest Level!

Make up your mind you are going to live at the highest level for your life. You've heard this statement many times before; "these will be some of the **best** of times and the **worst** of times." What is the determining factor? The deciding factor is our choices. These determine God's reaction if we receive favor or judgment (see **Deuteronomy 30:19**) and only as we seek first the Kingdom of God, will all our other plans fall into proper place (see **Matthew 6:33**). Make it a top priority to spend time with God (see **Psalms 46:10-11**).

Knowing the Seasons
We can never clearly discern and understand the season we are in by what we observe in the natural. If you are walking merely by natural eyesight, you will find these are very distressing and dangerous dark days. However, if you will begin to walk by faith with steadfast confidence

in God (see **2 Corinthians 5:7**), you will begin to grasp the truth, amid all these things, we are *super overcomers* (see **Romans 8:37**).

Even in the center of chaos and turmoil, we are victorious because God is working all things for our good (see **Romans 8:28**)! Truly, when we let God's Spirit direct our life:

"To everything there is a season, and a time for every matter or purpose under heaven"
— **Ecclesiastes 3:1 (AMPC)**

It is imperative that we seek to walk in the revealed light of the Word of God (see **Psalms 119:130**). Make it your personal goal to walk with Divine purpose (see **Ephesians 5:14-18**), this is not a time to be lackadaisical or double-minded (see **James 1:8**). The greatest need in the Body of Christ is clear guidance.

No Real Wisdom and Common Sense without Holy Spirit Guidance!

Today scientific brilliance and spiritual blindness are a frightening union. By its restless cleverness, the mind of man, devoid of Holy Spirit guidance, has brought upon us a world situation just about beyond the limits of its own comprehension to control. You can never solve the problems of man with mere human cleverness. Scripture warns, ever learning and never able to come to the

CONCLUSION

knowledge of God (see **2 Timothy 3:7**). Never was a question more anxiously asked: "where are we going?"

Remember, what Christ Jesus taught when the blind lead the blind, both are destined to fall into the ditch (see **Matthew 15:14**)! Our greatest need is total dependence upon God's direction.

The holy Word of God, the Bible answers our questions: *Yes, there is clear, effective guidance for our pathway if only we will choose to walk in God's way.*

Make this clear and positive declaration:

"...But as for me and my house, we will serve the Lord."
—Joshua 24:15 (NKJV)

I pray the eyes of your heart will be flooded with revelatory light as you study this book and its corresponding scriptures (see **Ephesians 1:18**). May the Lord give you wisdom and insight as you seek His face (see **Psalm 27:8**)!

Amen!

Bobby Conner

Eagles View Ministries

RESOURCES

BOBBY CONNER
Eagles View Ministries

SHEPHERD'S ROD
VOLUME XXIII

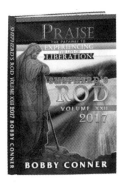

**PRAISE
THE PATHWAY TO
EXPERIENCING THE LIFE OF
LIBERATION**

In this 2017 Shepherd's Rod, you will discover extremely powerful and productive weapons for waging successful spiritual warfare against the adversary of your soul. God has given us powerful weapons to drive the devil back and to bind his power.

One such weapon is the action of praise; it is not a drudgery but rather a delightful principle that will unlock the pathway to living a liberated life. Time is too short, we don't have another moment to waste, we must take advantage of every opportunity and make the most of each day.

**BOBBY CONNER
Eagles View Ministries
www.BobbyConner.org**
PO BOX 933, BULLARD, TEXAS 75757

RESOURCES

BOBBY CONNER
EaglesViewMinistries

MASTER'S PLAN
2ND EDITION AMPLIFIED VERSION

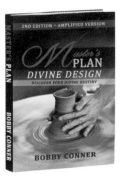

WHAT IS HIS DIVINE DESIGN FOR YOUR LIFE?

Think about it! You are Divinely unique, no other human on earth is like you! Amid the seven billion plus people alive on this planet God has made only one you. One of the criteria for placing value on an object is how rare is it? You were chosen by God in eternity past, to live in the present, to forge the future.

Packed within these 237 pages you will discover truths that will aid you in unlocking your Divine Destiny, discovering the reason you were given life!

BOBBY CONNER
EaglesViewMinistries
www.BobbyConner.org
PO BOX 933, BULLARD, TEXAS 75757

RESOURCES

BOBBY CONNER
EaglesViewMinistries

LINEAGE-LINE AND LEGACY
REVISED 2ND EDITION

WITHIN THESE PAGES YOU WILL DISCOVER NUMEROUS FRESH NEW INSIGHTS TO ASSIST YOU IN YOUR JOURNEY.

You will be guided and directed how to release God's Divine spoken blessing over yourself as well as your descendants. You will discover the power to break family curses. Each one of us has been given a priceless gift—the power to influence lives.

It is a proven fact our lives can be the building blocks for overwhelming success or the stumbling stones for coming generations. Take heart, even if you have failed in the past to present a positive encouraging example, it is never too late.

BOBBY CONNER
EaglesViewMinistries
www.BobbyConner.org
PO BOX 933, BULLARD, TEXAS 75757

RESOURCES

BOBBY CONNER
EaglesViewMinistries

LIVING IN GOD'S LIGHT
UNCERTAIN TIMES

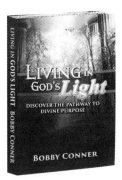

Within these pages you will discover inspirational insights; these truths have the potential to radically transform your life.

These life lessons will release hope and impart courage and confidence giving you guidelines revealing how to best position yourselves to obtain God's perfect plans and purposes for your life.

This book will aid you as a seeker of Divine Truth to dig ever deeper into the treasures of God's Word, thus obtaining the wonderful promises that will release to you steadfastness and confidence to face uncertain times.

BOBBY CONNER
EaglesViewMinistries
www.BobbyConner.org
PO BOX 933, BULLARD, TEXAS 75757

RESOURCES

BOBBY CONNER
EaglesViewMinistries

HEAVENS HOST
THE ASSIGNMENTS OF ANGELS

Who are Heaven's Host and what are their assignments?

In our modern society, many scoff at the reality of angels and demons or even the existence of the   supernatural. However, to remain uninformed   concerning such issues could prove to be extremely costly.

The company of angels is as vast as God's creation. If you believe the Bible, you will believe in their mission and ministry.

The forces of light and dark, good and evil, are on a collision course, and it is imperative that the saints of God prepare for the conflict!

BOBBY CONNER
EaglesViewMinistries
www.BobbyConner.org
PO BOX 933, BULLARD, TEXAS 75757

RESOURCES

BOBBY CONNER
Eagles View Ministries

EMPOWERED BY GOD

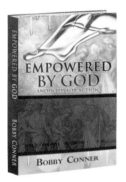

You are called and commissioned to walk in Kingdom authority and power! As a follower of Christ Jesus you are expected to accomplish the same supernatural works He did even greater.

This book will aid you in realizing how to embrace the process and purpose of spiritual character and maturity, the importance of investing your life into the kingdom.

It is time to exit the pathway of apathy and advance in the journey to divine empowerment becoming a spiritual revolutionary ready to shape the future!

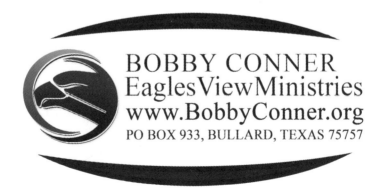

BOBBY CONNER
Eagles View Ministries
www.BobbyConner.org
PO BOX 933, BULLARD, TEXAS 75757